Gold in the
Ashes

GOLD IN THE ASHES

MICHELLE BOOTH

VICTOR BOOKS

A DIVISION OF SCRIPTURE PRESS PUBLICATIONS INC.
USA CANADA ENGLAND

Scripture quotations are from the *New American Standard Bible*, ©
the Lockman Foundation 1960, 1962, 1963, 1968, 1971, 1972, 1973,
1975, 1977.

Editor: Carolyn Nystrom
Cover Design: Mardelle Ayres
Photographer: William Koechling

Recommended Dewey Decimal Classification: 223:1
Suggested Subject Headings: BIBLE, O.T., JOB

Library of Congress Catalog Card Number: 93-16926
ISBN: 1-56476-050-2

1 2 3 4 5 6 7 8 9 10 Printing/Year 97 96 95 94 93

VICTOR BOOKS
A division of SP Publications, Inc.
Wheaton, Illinois 60187

CONTENTS

To Ellen Martinez,
for being a faithful friend
through my fiery ordeals
and helping me to find
gold in my ashes.

INTRODUCTION

We live in a suffering world. At times, circumstances crush us in the rubble. At other times, depression engulfs a friend. How does God want us to handle such sorrow? We must hang onto our faith. But how? God's Word is a lifeline. In it, God teaches us what He expects of us and how we can go about living it out. He shows us how to cling to Him and how to help others draw to Him. This is wisdom.

Scripture often speaks of wisdom as "gold." It speaks of the refinement process: fire to burn off the impurities. It speaks of the result of these painful trials: the pure gold of faith.

We might expect life's adversities to cause us to reject God. But, in fact, quite the opposite can occur. The Apostle Peter wrote, ". . .you have been distressed by various trials, that the proof of your faith, being more precious than gold which is perishable, even though tested by fire, may be found to result in praise and glory and honor at the revelation of Jesus Christ. (1 Peter 1:6-7)

GOLD IN THE ASHES is a tool to help us glean wisdom to pass our tests of fire. We can use this guide either for individual study or for group discussion. In it, we will follow the theme of processing gold as we study one of history's greatest books about suffering: the Book of Job.

Each chapter of this study guide will be divided into four parts.

🐾 **Sifting for Nuggets** is a section of Scripture references and Bible study questions from the Book of Job. This section will deepen your understanding of the Scriptures and will help you think of creative ways to make its teachings a part of your own way of living. If you are discussing this book with a group, use this section as your personal preparation for the time of group discussion.

🐾 **Staking a Claim** is a devotional narrative to help clarify and expand what you learned in the study questions. It will give background information, demonstrate the harmony between Job and the rest of the Bible, and describe how the Scriptures relate to real-life situations. Read this section before you attend your group meeting. You may also reread and discuss parts of it with your group.

🐛 **Taking It Home** is a list of optional activities to help you practice newly learned truths in your daily life.

🐛 **Refinement** is a list of suggested prayers on the subject of the study. It will include prayer topics, Scriptures for meditation, and prayable passages.

Who actually penned the Book of Job? Scholars are not sure. But like all Scripture, it was inspired by our Holy God. The account of Job's life contains nuggets of gold hidden in the dirt and ashes of human advice. As we read Job's story of fiery trials and get a glimpse into his heart, we can gain infinite insight into what it means to faithfully endure. As we live these truths, we can pray for the ability to say as Job did:

When He has tried me, I shall come forth as gold (Job 23:10).

THE BOOK OF JOB

Chapters	1–2	3	4–14	15–21	22–31	32–37	38–41	42
Job's Situation	Satan's Scheme (Job Is Tested)	Dialogue Begins	Cycle 1 of Debate	Cycle 2 of Debate	Cycle 3 of Debate	Elihu Speaks	God Speaks	Job Is Restored
			Job Is Counseled by Men					
Job's Responses	Job Trusts in God	Job Despairs	Job Tries to Vindicate Himself			Job Learns	Job Is Humbled	Job Repents
						Job Listens		

SATAN'S BATTLE, GOD'S WAR

SIFTING FOR NUGGETS

1. Read Job 1:1–2:13. Describe Job in your own terms.

2. What type of parent do you think he was?

3. Job loved his children deeply and went to great pains to bring them to God. Describe how someone you know has shown that type of love.

4. Look more carefully at Job 1:6-22. Why hadn't Satan attacked Job before?

5. In Satan's opinion, why did Job serve God?

6. How did the messengers coming in rapid succession work in Satan's favor?

7. We often say, "When it rains it pours." We all go through times when it feels like our entire world is crumbling. These are acute trials. But other trials keep nagging through time, causing battle fatigue. These are chronic trials. How did Job respond to the acute trial described in chapter 1?

8. Read again Job 1:20 and 2:12. In Old Testament times, people expressed mourning in graphic ways. They tore their clothes, shaved their heads, fell to the ground, rolled in ashes, moaned, and chanted. Our culture no longer includes these outward expressions of emotion. If you were extremely upset or sorrowful, and no one was watching, how might you creatively express and release your feelings?

9. Study Job 2:1-6. Was God satisfied with Job's performance in the first battle?

10. What was Satan's way of subtly discounting Job's victory?

11. Study Job 2:7-10. How did Job's first and second reactions differ?

12. All of Job's children died. We know that his wife was spared because her conversation with her husband is recorded in Job 2:9-10. Read this interchange again. Why do you think Satan spared Job's wife?

13. Satan made a strong attack in chapters 1 and 2. Then, in the following 23 chapters, Job's friends argue with him about his integrity. Use the trials of Job to fill in the following chart.

	TRIALS	CHRONIC OR ACUTE
POSSESSIONS		
PHYSICAL WELL-BEING		
PERSONAL RELATIONSHIPS		

14. Now think of your own present or past trials. Then fill in the following chart.

	TRIALS	CHRONIC OR ACUTE
POSSESSIONS		
PHYSICAL WELL-BEING		
PERSONAL RELATIONSHIPS		

15. Survey again Job's response thus far to the tragedy that has plagued him. What do you hope will be a part of your own response the next time you face a trial?

16. How is that different from your past responses?

17. None of us can expect a life free of hardship. What are some steps that you can take now to prepare yourself for your next period of suffering?

STAKING A CLAIM

Nowhere in Scripture are Satan's techniques described in more detail than in the first two chapters of the Book of Job. Satan saunters into the throne room of the Lord. There, he nonchalantly informs the Almighty that he has been roaming about the earth, obviously in search of someone to pester. The next verse surprises and horrifies us. God *suggests* that Satan try Job! Poor blameless and upright Job suddenly has a large bull's-eye placed on his head for the devil's missiles!

From Job's point of view this all looks pretty unfair. But let's try to look at the plan from a heavenly perspective. Satan was going to test someone. Job was no pawn in some heavenly game—he was God's best warrior in the holy war. God knew Job's strengths and limitations; He was sure that He and Job could win the battle. God was in control. He let Satan test Job relentlessly. But notice that Satan could not exceed the restrictions God imposed on him. Satan may have been granted free rein for a time, but God had complete reign over him at all times.

For the past fifteen years, I have struggled with consistent headaches. There are many nights when I cry to the Lord that I cannot endure another day of pain. The next morning, when I feel as though my skull has a railroad spike driven through it, I sometimes wish I hadn't awakened. The Lord, however, gives me grace not only to survive, but to love and serve my children. He knows my limits better than I do. He also, by His mercy, gives me days or weeks without pain. I am learning to trust God to keep Satan outside my limits of endurance, and to stay with me in my pain to help me grow.

God does His part to restrain Satan, but we must resist him. The Bible instructs us to be ready for Satan's attacks. First Peter 5:8-10 states:

> Be sober of *spirit*, be on the alert. Your adversary, the devil, prowls about like a roaring lion, seeking someone to devour. But resist him, firm in *your* faith, knowing that the same experiences of suffering are being accomplished by your brethren who are in the world. And after you have suffered for a little, the God of all grace, who called you to His eternal glory in Christ, will Himself perfect, confirm, strengthen, *and* establish you.

What a victorious passage! As long as we resist the devil and remain firm in our faith, God Himself will be the victor. He will make us perfect and establish us firmly in His kingdom beyond the reach of Satan! So, how do we resist Satan and stand firm in our faith? Let's look back at how Job was prepared for the attack. He habitually resisted Satan by "turning away from evil" (Job 1:1). In this way he was "blameless and upright." As for being firm in his faith, Job had an awesome respect for God (Job 1:1, 20-21). He saw the importance of consecrating himself and his family before the Lord. He did this by way of a sacrificial offering. We can be consecrated by accepting Jesus, God's ultimate sacrifice for sin, and confessing to Him regularly.

We find the key factor in Job's favor in Job 1:5: "Thus Job did continually." He had good times and bad times, but his faith was continuous. Somewhere along the line, Job had decided to always stand firm for God. Have you taken that step? It is a hard decision to make, and it is harder yet to keep, but the rewards are worth the struggle. We must set up our camp deep in the territory of the Victor, but be ready to go to the front line with Him when necessary.

You may say, "Job was stronger; he was right out of the Bible." Wrong. Job didn't have nearly the strength nor the protection that you and I have available to us today. Before Jesus came, people could not experience the cleansing and indwelling of the Holy Spirit as we can. Whether Christian moms or grandmas, nurses or business women, we have the power of the Almighty God within us. If we truly draw on the power of the Holy Spirit, we can vanquish Satan no matter what missiles he shoots our way! So let's study Job as a human being, God as the Almighty, and ourselves as who we are—and as who we can be in Jesus.

Taking it home

Use one or more of the following suggestions to gain more insight on the spiritual battles that you encounter.

1. Think of a chronic trial that you are experiencing in your life. It can be as small as laundry or diapers, as overwhelming as divorce, as wearing as constant pain, or as troublesome as financial problems. Write 1 Peter 5:10 on an index card and place it on your refrigerator or your bathroom mirror. This week, try to DAILY read this verse and ask God to begin His process of perfecting, confirming, strengthening, and establishing you.

2. Draw a large heart on a piece of paper. Think of this drawing as a military map of your spiritual battleground. Divide it into eight to ten "countries." Read Galatians 5:19-23 for ideas of areas that Satan would like to fight for in your life. Label each "country" as one of these areas. At the beginning of each day this week, pray that God will strengthen and protect you in each of the areas. At the end of each day, reexamine your map. If you feel that the Lord triumphed through you in an area, put a plus sign. If you feel that you lost ground, put a minus. On the last day, read Philippians

1:6. Go back to your map and put a large plus sign (or cross) in each area to show how the war will end when you are in heaven with Christ.

3. Read the following passages and write a paragraph or two on Satan's standing in God's realm in the past, present, and future. Then write God a specific thank-you note.

PAST
Isaiah 14:12-14
Genesis 3:1-4

PRESENT
Genesis 3:14-15
John 12:30-33
John 17:15

FUTURE
Revelation 12:10-11
Revelation 20:1-2, 10

REFINEMENT

Pray. Select patterns for prayer from these suggestions.
1. Read Ephesians 6:14-17. Ask God specifically to help you learn to use each piece of armor.
2. If you are experiencing suffering, read Psalm 6 as a prayer.
3. Pray for believers you know who are going through trials. Ask God to strengthen them.
4. Pray for strength for yourself and praise God for His control over your life and over Satan.

SEARCHING FOR REASONS

Sifting for Nuggets

1. On a separate piece of paper or in the back of this book, write the numbers 1-42 in column form. Chapters 1, 2, and 42 are narration. The others are speeches. Look at the first two verses of each chapter to discover the speaker. Then note these on your chart. If the first or second verse doesn't name a speaker, the chapter is merely a continuation of an earlier speech. What patterns do you see?

2. Now quickly read the entire book. Pencil notes in the margin that will help you spot the major point of each speech.

3. Read Job 2:5. What was Satan's reason for plaguing Job?

4. Read Job 2:9. What did Job's wife want him to do?

5. In view of his wife's instructions to Job, what did she seem to see as the reason for his trial?

6. Job's wife suffered almost as much as Job did. How did their attitudes differ?

7. What do you think would have happened if Job had followed her advice?

8. Three factors in our response to trials are: our view of the reason, our view of God, and our view of what we should do. Fill in the chart below to discover the point of view of each speech.

	Job 4:7-9	Job 5:17-18	Job 8:4-6	Job 11:4-6, 13-15
❦ the speaker				
❦ the reason				
❦ the view of God				
❦ what Job should do				

9. Some of the views offered to Job were at least partially correct, but no one seemed to see the whole picture. After listening to the conflicting views of others, Job may have begun to lose sight of his own concept of God. In Job 9 and 10, Job expresses a variety of pictures of God. Answer each question below citing several verses from Job 9 and 10.

❦ What reasons does Job see for his many troubles?

❦ What is his concept of God?

❦ What does Job think he should do?

10. A first impulse to suffering is to "find a reason." We mistakenly think that if we can find God's reasons for our awful pain, we can accept what has happened to us. But our eyesight is as limited as the sight of Job and his friends. Instead, we must change our emphasis from searching for reasons to cooperating with God's will for us. Below is a list of positive outcomes (not reasons) that God brought about in the Book of Job. Read the Scriptures and write each reference on the chart next to the outcome that the verse describes. (Answers may vary.) Even if the reason eludes us, we can still accept the good that can come from suffering.
    ❦ Job 12:5 compared to Job 16:1-5
    ❦ Job 17:7-9
    ❦ Job 33:29-30
    ❦ Job 38:1-7
    ❦ Job 42:5-6
    ❦ Job 42:7-9

OUTCOMES	VERSE
DISCIPLINE (correction for past sins)	
DIRECTION (turning to God for enlightenment)	
DEVELOPMENT OF MINISTRY (one who has suffered empathizes)	
DEEPENING OF FAITH (new level of awareness of God)	
DEMONSTRATION (God showing His victory in heaven or earth)	
DRAMA (people watching the scene learn from it)	

11. Read Job 38:1-7. We will study God's entire speech later, but His introduction is indicative of His whole speech. Does God seem inclined to answer Job's "why" question with a reason?

12. Job's speeches and actions demonstrate an amazing openness. We see his struggles as well as his victories, his faults as well as his strengths. Describe the extent to which you are open and honest with others during times of trials.

13. Job states in Job 19:23-24:

> Oh that my words were written!
> Oh that they were inscribed in a book!
> That with an iron stylus and lead
> They were engraved in a rock forever!

Job didn't know that God would actually write them in a book. God chose to unfold Job's story completely (demonstrating human weakness and heavenly workings) into His Holy Word which lasts forever. As a result, we can all benefit from the lessons Job learned. Write down any new perspectives you have gained on trials so far in this study.

STAKING A CLAIM

The Sound of Music is a favorite movie to many families. It embodies all that we feel life should be; good triumphs over evil, hard hearts are softened, and love is the victor. We follow this tender and humorous love story as it works its way to the dramatic climax in Baron von Trapp's garden. He and his beautiful governess finally express their love for each other and begin to embrace. As we expectantly await the sealing kiss, Julie Andrews tilts her head back and sings, "Somewhere in my youth or childhood I must have done something good."

Because we are creatures of reason, we feel that there must be a cause for everything. When we encounter suffering, our response is to tilt our head back and release an anguished cry to the heavens such as, "Why me, God? What did I ever do to deserve this?" We don't actually expect an answer to boom forth from the clouds, yet the question torments our souls to such an extent that we are compelled to ask it.

The "why" question is the driving force behind most of the human dialogue in the Book of Job. Eliphaz felt that Job was being disciplined for his past sins (Job 5:17; 22:5, 21). Bildad felt that God is an administrator of justice on earth and that Job must have deserved what he received (Job 8:5-6). Zophar claimed that if Job were to stop being so sinful, his troubles would pass (Job 11:14-17). But Job was insulted by his friends' poor use of human logic.

Have you ever had a friend "help" you by attempting to explain your trial? She begins, "I don't know how to say this but. . . ." Or, "I was thinking about why God would let this sort of thing happen. . . ." She sits there, coffee in hand, trying desperately to enlighten you or at least to get you thinking. What you are thinking is, "Won't she ever go home?" Finally, your preacher-friend wraps up her sermon (without benediction) and leaves. You breathe a sigh of relief.

But after your friend leaves, her words continue to haunt you. What if she is right? The agony of your first "why cry" to God returns. You search your past for sins or lessons unlearned. Soul searching and confession are vital—but not for the purpose of finding reasons that God could be punishing us. Such sin searches, with expectations of ending a trial by passing a test, are frustrating and futile. We should accept God's forgiveness and reserve our emotional energy for growing through our trials.

Of all the humans who attempted to enlighten Job, Elihu came the closest. He had endured days of debate between Job and the three friends. He had listened to the closing arguments of Job's final speech. Elihu then stated the opinion that God is a sovereign God who has many reasons for His actions. It is not for us to critique the plot, but to trust in the Author of our salvation. Elihu stated that, "Whether for correction, or for His world, or for lovingkindness, He causes it to happen" (Job 37:13). What amazing insight!

Elihu may have had more to say, but we will never know. Suddenly, the drum roll of thunder caught everyone's attention. The house lights dimmed. Bolts of lightning attracted all eyes to the heavenly stage. God entered in a storm cloud. The audience, after enduring hours of human speculation, thrilled. God really WAS going to boom an answer from the clouds!

The voice from the whirlwind must have shaken Job as God bellowed, "Who is this that darkens counsel by words without knowledge? Where were you when I laid the foundations of the earth? Will the faultfinder contend with the Almighty!" (Job 38:2, 4; 40:2) Job was humbled and repentant. He realized that he was not haggling with some livestock dealer over a speckled lamb, but was demanding an audience with the sovereign God of the universe. After revelation from God, "why" became irrelevant.

In the end, Job was a happy and wise man who was at peace with his God and his family. But that too is a minor addendum to the story. More important, is Job's (and our) understanding of the character of God. Job never did understand why God allowed his devastation. God never told him. Ten new children would never replace the ones who died. (Ask any parent who has lost a child.) But Job had encountered the Almighty Living God. After that Job put his hand over his mouth.

So what does this mean to us? It means that we can change our emphasis in trials from the search for reasons to the search for outcomes. We are instructed in James 1:2-3 to "Consider it all joy, my brethren, when you encounter various trials, knowing that the testing of your faith produces endurance. And let endurance have its perfect result, that you may be perfect and complete, lacking in nothing." Considering trials joy may seem impossible. But if we cease striving in our search for why, and fix our eyes on the character of God, we may begin to see some of the perfect results that James promises. If we start asking God how to use us for His glory, we can start our growth process toward completeness. So let's change our "whys" to "hows" and change our cries to bows of reverence, and watch God's hand at work.

TAKING IT HOME

Choose one or more of the following activities to help you to apply the principle of cooperating with God for good outcomes this week.

1. Think of a hardship that you have experienced in the past. Fill out the chart below to show some of your own steps in personal growth. Then show what (if anything) you learned about God.

My past trial was: _____

OUTCOMES	NEW INSIGHTS INTO GOD'S CHARACTER	PERSONAL GROWTH
DISCIPLINE		
DIRECTION		
DEVELOPMENT OF MINISTRY		
DEEPENED FAITH		
DEMONSTRATION		
DRAMA		

2. Fill out the chart on page 24 with a present trial and think of how you could cooperate so that God will have free reign to bring about His own purposes.

My present trial is: _____

3. Meet with God in the morning each day this week. Ask Him to show you a way that you could obey His will for you that day. Next, spend at least five minutes in prayer or silence. Be sensitive to His Spirit. Then look for opportunities to serve Him during the day—even if you are experiencing trials. In the evening, think about the following questions. Did I cooperate with God to the best of my abilities? If God were to ask me why I did some of the things that I did today, what might He ask? What would I answer? Record events below that nudged you toward spiritual growth.

POSSIBLE OUTCOME	HOW I COULD COOPERATE
DISCIPLINE	
DIRECTION	
DEVELOPMENT	
DEEPENED FAITH	
DEMONSTRATION	
DRAMA	

REFINEMENT

The following are suggestions for prayer:

1. Meditate on these words from Job 37:13: "Whether for correction, or for His world, or for lovingkindness, He causes it to happen." Pray that God will use your suffering for His glory.

2. If you are presently suffering, try the following suggestion. Hebrews 5:8 says this about Jesus: "Although He was a Son, He learned obedience from the things which He suffered." In Gethsemane, Jesus struggled with submission to God's will for His crucifixion. Read Christ's prayer in Mark 14:36. If you are able, rewrite this prayer as it fits your own current suffering. Then pray it to your loving Father.

3. Pray for friends who are suffering and struggling with questions and confusion. Pray that the Lord will bring them to trust in His wisdom and power.

4. Pray for yourself that God will make you aware of people who depend on you as an example of faith during trial. Pray that the Lord will give you the strength and peace to be transparent so that they can see God at work in you.

3

SINKING INTO DESPAIR

Sifting for Nuggets

1. We all experience trials. Some seem bearable, and some do not. List conditions that make a trial seem too much to accept.

2. What kinds of help do you look for during a period of suffering?

3. Read Job 1:20-21 and 2:10. Write down words from the text that show Job's main actions after each of the two stages of this trial.

4. Read Job 3. Write down repeated words, phrases, or thoughts that express Job's frame of mind.

5. Which (if any) of these have you ever felt?

6. Read Job 6:8-13. Job states in verse 10 that he has succeeded in his faith so far since he has not "denied the words of the Holy One." What is Job's wish, and what is his worry?

7. Scan chapters 7, 9, 10, and 21 and look for question marks. (These are all portions of Job's speeches.) Read the questions that Job asks. How would you describe his frame of mind during this portion of his trial?

8. The key questions in Job's heart revolved around God's character. Read the following verses, and write them in the format of an "Are You?" question to God (Are You loving? Are You worthy? etc.).

Job 7:21

Job 9:19

Job 10:3

Job 21:15

9. Have you ever questioned the reality of any of the attributes of God? If so, which ones?

10. Job, like us, had a finite mind. He couldn't reconcile God's love and justice with his own unexplained ordeal. His legitimate emotional state made it difficult to cling to his previously unquestioned view of God. Read the following sections to get a glimpse of his inner turmoil: Job 9:5–10:7; Job 23:8-17; and Job 30:18-23. Write a few lines of how you think Job would have described God during this stage. Try to include what Job thought of God's personality, actions, and perception of His people.

11. In spite of his pain, Job was still aware of God's power (Job 9:19). Have you ever felt that a situation was too much for even God to handle? What evidence, if any, did you see of God's power during that time?

12. What is the difference between fair and just?

13. Read Job 32:2 and 33:8-12. What does Elihu accuse Job of?

14. Read Job 38:1-2 and 40:1-2. What does God accuse Job of?

15. Job met the challenge of Satan. During the ordeal he brought his thoughts (even if rash) to God. In times of pain, we can offend someone or sin against that person without severing the relationship. If you were Job, what (if anything) would you have confessed to God?

16. Read Job 42:10-17. How would you describe God's final dealings with Job?

17. Verse 16 says that Job saw his sons and his grandsons to the fourth generation. What do you think that he told them about the trial era of his life?

18. What would you want your descendants or close friends to learn from your own trials?

STAKING A CLAIM

What could be worse than not knowing the Lord? To know Him and to deny Him.

Many men and women through the ages have confessed faith in Christ and later failed to follow Him. The reason was usually that their circumstances were not what they felt believers deserved. They couldn't reconcile their faith in God with the circumstances of their lives, so they stopped believing. Yet only their faith could have reconciled them to God for eternal life. The cause was calamity; the effect was catastrophe.

What could cause a Christian to sink into despair to the extent of denying her faith? Is it a plunge or a process? It seems to happen in stages. Job started his journey of suffering as an upright and blameless man. In the end God called him to repent. We will look at his process using the acrostic P.A.I.N.

Praise
Acceptance
Inner Struggle
Negative Image of God

Praise
Job's initial reaction to the catastrophic death of his children and animals was to praise God. What an incredible faith! Not many of us respond to anguish with adoration. Job fell on his face, worshiped, and blessed the name of the Lord (Job 1:20-22).

Acceptance
Job's second trial was physical illness. This was a painful disease involving itchy ulcerous sores (Job 2:7-8), loss of appetite (Job 3:24), hardened skin (Job 30:30), and constant pain (Job 30:17). Job's reaction to this second trial was to accept. He stated to his wife, "Shall we indeed accept good from God and not accept adversity?" (Job 2:10) He no longer worshiped, but he gritted his teeth and submitted to his sovereign Lord. Sometimes, even though our souls feel unable to rise to the spiritual peak of praise, we can still remain on the plateau of obedience. This type of submission requires a deep belief that God is in control and is doing what is best. We know less of Job's heart reaction to the second trial. God does state, however, that Job did not sin with his lips. Acceptance is acceptable.

Inner Struggle
Job's inner struggle came with his third trial, a trial brought on by his friends. Job's friends attacked his integrity. They set up the dangerous logic in their first speeches: God is just and punishes the wicked, therefore Job is sinful. This put the truth of God's justice in juxtaposition to the reality of Job's righteousness. Job's view of God was put to the test as his agonized mind churned in turmoil. He still believed in God's greatness and sovereignty (Job 9:4-12). He just needed answers to the questions roaring through his head. Would God listen to him? (Job 9:16) Could he receive justice from God? (Job 9:19) Does God cause unfairness in this world? (Job 9:24) How could God love him and still impose unfair punishment on him? (Job 10:12-17)

Negative Image of God
The catastrophe had left an imprint on the film of Job's mind. Job

struggled to maintain an accurate image of God in a darkroom of debate where everything was seen in black and white. His thoughts were trapped in the utter darkness of despair. Ideas swirled in baths of pain and confusion. His mind struggled to fix his picture of God to the image of the catastrophe to which his mind had been exposed. His friends offered no solutions. In this photographic process, his view of God sometimes changed from positive to negative and back to positive again. Job exclaimed that God is "wise in heart and mighty in strength" (Job 9:4). In the same chapter, he claimed that God hurt him without cause (Job 9:17) and that He "mocks the despair of the innocent" (Job 9:23). Job stated that there is no justice (Job 19:7) and that God had considered him an enemy (Job 19:11). Yet these assertions came in the same speech as his confident exclamation of "I know that my Redeemer lives" (Job 19:25).

All of us have an imperfect view of God. In times of turmoil, we too may create for ourselves a negative image of God. This is a dangerous stage. It is here that many deny their faith in God because of a false image which exists only in the darkroom of their confused minds. Job did not do this. He kept trying until he had a clear image of the living God. Once this happened, he saw the need to repent of the sins he had committed during the process. He had gone so far as to accuse God of being cruel and of persecuting him (Job 30:21). When we come out of our dark times, we too may need to confess.

My husband and I sometimes have angry discussions. I say things I should not say. But voicing these statements sometimes reveals to me how ridicuous they are. Afterward, when I have time alone to calm down, I realize that I don't agree with what I said. It is then that I recognize the need to apologize. The same happens after moments of anger with my Lord. I, like Job, must confess my sin.

We can find comfort in God's tough/tender correction. Elihu said, "God thunders with His voice wonderously," (Job 37:5). When our majestic God uses His "Ahem . . ." scolding voice, it is a storm, yet He is merciful. The Lord humbled, but didn't humiliate Job. He rebuked, but later rewarded him. He demonstrated His power, but didn't punish. Above all, God is love.

We may ask, "How do I keep from following these stages? Do I sink into sin as soon as I stop praising?" Definitely not. The key stage in the turmoil that accompanies suffering is the inner struggle. When we begin to question God's more endearing attributes, we must go about it with respect.

Job never denied God's existence, nor did he stop looking for answers to his questions. Job was involved in a spiritual wrestling match begging God to speak. Job did not forfeit the match through absence or through a belief that God was absent. He wrestled with his faith until God won and Job was content. We can struggle with our faith, but we must keep God in our struggles.

If our questions cause us to seek to know what God is like, these questions can become an avenue of growth. As we seek God, we will find Him to be worthy of our faith. From here, we can again accept. As we see God for who He truly is, praise is a natural reaction.

Today, we have resources that would have delighted Job: The Bible explains God as deeply as we can comprehend Him. We have Jesus as a picture of God's character. The Holy Spirit teaches us through the enlightening of the Word and through prayer. We have churches, pastors, and Christian books. Our responsibility, in happy times and in pain, is to use these resources to continue to seek God. As long as we cling to Him, and don't deny Him, we can question our faithful God who promises:

If we endure,
we shall also reign with Him;
If we deny Him,
He also will deny us;
If we are faithless,
He remains faithful;
for He cannot deny Himself.
    —2 Timothy 2:12-13

TAKING IT HOME

Choose one or more of the following ideas to help you examine your view of God and how you respond to Him.
1. It is good to examine our faith and to identify our strong and weak areas. In this exercise, we will look at our view of who God is. Divide a large piece of paper into three columns. Write the word GOD at the top of the paper, placing one letter at the top of each column. Read the following list which names some of the attributes of God. Think about each attribute and decide how

strongly you believe in your heart (not your head), that it accurately describes the Lord. If you are "good" at seeing God in that light, put that word in the column under the "G." If you have "difficulty" seeing God in that way, place the word in the column under the "D." If you "occasionally" see God as having that attribute (depending on your circumstances), place that word in the column under the "O."

Active (Hebrews 4:12)	Healer (Psalm 103:3)
All-knowing (Psalm 139:1-6)	Holy (1 Peter 1:14-16)
Almighty (Revelation 19:6)	Independent (Isaiah 40:13-14)
Awesome (Psalm 89:6-7)	Just (Psalm 19:9)
Blameless (Psalm 18:30)	Kind (Psalm 100:5)
Caring (1 Peter 5:6-7)	Loving (1 John 4:8)
Comforting (Isaiah 51:12)	Majestic (Psalm 8:1)
Compassionate (Psalm 103:8)	Merciful (Psalm 86:15)
Creator (Genesis 1:1)	Patient (2 Peter 3:9)
Delight, Able to (Psalm 37:23)	Peace Loving (Judges 6:23-24)
Disciplinarian (Revelation 3:19)	Protective (Psalm 121:7-8)
Eternal (Psalm 90:2)	Righteous (Psalm 11:7)
Everywhere (Psalm 139:7-10)	Sovereign (Psalm 103:19)
Faithful (Hebrews 10:23)	Tenderhearted (Luke 1:76-79)
Forgiving (1 John 1:9)	Unchanging (Malachi 3:6)
Gentle (Psalm 18:35)	Wise (Isaiah 28:29)

Take stock of the chart you have created. Praise God for all of His attributes that have become a part of your own heart-song. For those qualities that are still more a part of your head than your heart, ask God to continue to reveal Himself to you in ways that you can fully apprehend.

2. Think back on your last period of suffering. Read question 15 in the *Sifting for Nuggets* section. Think of ways you may have sinned against God or offended Him. Confess those sins to Him and thank Him for His mercy and forgiveness.

3. Sometimes we feel that our attitude is so bad that we can't come into God's presence. Many of the psalms disclose the feelings of authors with astounding openness. God did not discard the prayers of these men. Instead, He wrote their prayers in the Bible to be treasured forever. If you think that your feelings toward God are so bitter that prayer is impossible, read the following psalms as

prayers. Read them in order, one each day. Try to accept the fact that God is not offended by your feelings. As the prayers change during the week, try to make the statements of worship in these psalms your own hymn of praise.

- Psalm 88
- Psalm 77
- Psalm 42
- Psalm 31
- Psalm 6
- Psalm 56
- Psalm 5

REFINEMENT

The following are suggestions for prayer:
1. The Spirit of God within us longs to praise Him. Read Psalm 43. Note in verse 5, that the psalmist's mind and soul seem to be in dispute, yet he promises to praise again. If your head-knowledge of God doesn't seem to match your feelings, read Psalm 43 again as a prayer.
2. If you have a friend who is in deep pain, pray for her. Pray for her circumstances to get easier. Pray that she will learn more about the Lord through her trial. Pray that her faith will be strengthened. Pray for wisdom to know how to be a friend to her.
3. Pray that you and each member of your study group may grow to know God more fully and deeply. Pray Ephesians 3:14-21 for each member by inserting her name in place of "you."
4. Praise God by reading Psalm 103 as a prayer. To personalize it, substitute "my" for "your" or "our." If this prayer is too difficult to pray sincerely, try suggestion 3 in *Taking It Home*.

4

SAVING OUR FAITH

Sifting for Nuggets

1. One of the characteristics of Job that makes him so endearing is that he didn't hide what happened in his heart. Read the following passages. What are some of the feelings Job expressed to his friends?

Job 16:16
Job 19:2-3
Job 21:3-6
Job 23:2

2. What inhibits us from being open with others during our difficult times?

3. The following verses contain parts of Job's prayers. What feelings does he express to the Lord?

Job 7:11-16
Job 9:27-31
Job 30:24-28

4. What inhibits us from being open with God?

5. What are some advantages of being open with God?

6. What were some of the obstacles Job had to overcome in order to seek God fervently?

   Job 13:14-15
   Job 23:3-9
   Job 23:13-17
   Job 30:20-23

7. What are some basic beliefs that Job never let go of?

   Job 10:12
   Job 12:13-18
   Job 19:25-27

8. What are some beliefs you feel you would never let go of?

9. Read Job 23:10-12. Job decided to remain obedient at all costs. In what ways is it harder to be obedient during trials?

10. When life gets hard, we often just survive and lose sight of the spiritual battle. Job did not. At one point, he narrowed his request to two things. What were they? (See Job 13:20-22.)

11. If you were allowed only two requests from God, what would they be?

12. Job was seeking God to the best of his ability given his situation. What are ways that we can seek God?

13. Read James 5:11. This description of Job is the summary of a paragraph on patience during suffering. What was Job patiently awaiting? (See Job 19:25-27.)

14. What hopes can we cling to that will help us endure?

STAKING A CLAIM

Part of God's refinement process for me has involved Ménière's disease. Because of this, I experience times of severely impaired equilibrium. This disability caused a backpacking trip to be one of my most terrifying experiences. My husband and I were traversing across a steep, rocky slope above an enormous cliff. With each step, rocks slid out from beneath my feet. As the slope slid beneath me, the entire world seemed to spin. It felt as if all the forces of gravity and hell were trying to suck me over the edge of the precipice.

As I lay sobbing into the stones, I looked up and saw a tree. It was the only immovable object on the slope, so I scrambled up to it with all my strength. I clung to the tree for nearly an hour (much to my husband's dismay). Finally, I began climbing again. At the top was a solid granite rock face. I made my way to safety clinging tightly to carefully chosen handholds in my rock wall. When my feet slipped, I never let go.

Job must have felt much as I did. He too looked up and put all of his energies into reaching his Rock of refuge, his God. Job was human and he slipped, but he clung to the Almighty. In so doing, he saved his faith. His ascent of faith suggests the acrostic H.I.G.H.:

Honest
Immovable Faith
God Seeking
Hushed

Honest
People are like tea kettles; we will self-destruct if there is no vent to blow off steam when the heat is on. The size of the vent affects the amount of pressure. Job chose God. He cried out:

I will give full vent to my complaint;
I will speak in the bitterness of my soul.
I will say to God, "Do not condemn me;
Let me know why Thou dost contend with me."
—Job 10:1-2

Job did not hide anything from God. He wept to God (Job 16:20). He vented his anguish (Job 7:11). He informed God of his fears as well as of his attempts to be cheerful (Job 9:27-28). Over half of Job's speeches turned into prayers. Job prayed through a long period of suffering silence before the Sovereign spoke.

It isn't easy to pray to God when we are angry with Him. To pray to a Heavenly Father who apparently forgot to protect us feels ridiculous. To pour our aching hearts out to a God who appears unresponsive seems futile, but we must do it to save our faith. God knows all. He isn't going to be shocked as we reveal ourselves. He is not unresponsive. As we open the lines of communication, He will reveal Himself.

The Lord's first response to Job's outspoken orations seemed harsh. But God did not rebuke Job for feeling angry, hurt, or desperate. He merely didn't want Job to be trying to find fault with Him. Our Heavenly Father longs for His children to be open with Him. He can handle our feelings. If His hand can powerfully alter the events of history, His shoulder is certainly big enough to cry on.

Immovable Faith

Rock climbers make very sure of their hand holds, for their lives depend on them. Our spiritual lives depend on the object of our faith. We must have some firm beliefs of which we will never let go. There must be some aspects of our belief in God, His Word, and salvation that we choose not to question. This way, if we begin to question some of the loftier aspects of our faith, we still have something to cling to.

During Job's speeches, he never lost sight of the fact that God is wise and in control (Job 9:4; 23:13-14; 28:24-28). He proclaimed to his friends: "With Him are wisdom and might; to Him belong counsel and understanding" (Job 12:13).

We often wish that we could control events in our lives, or at least know what the future holds. God, in His wisdom, has not chosen to give us this power. But we *do* have Someone who loves us dearly, knows all things, and controls all things. This is a much better alternative.

God Seeking

I felt safe as I clung to the tree. But to go on with life, I had to scramble, skin my knees, cut my hands, and exhaust myself to reach the rock. Life is painful. To sit passively with a mediocre faith isn't sufficient. You don't find many fence sitters on electric fences. If we have decided not to fall back in our faith, we must then go forward until we meet God face-to-face.

Job in his dauntless climb of faith said, "Even after my skin is flayed, yet without my flesh I shall see God" (Job 19:26). In one of his last speeches Job said that he had looked in every direction for God (Job 23:8-9). It is not that Job hadn't seen God in nature, but he wanted to see God Himself. Job got his desire (Job 42:5). This is one of the key purposes of trials. Against the stark background of having lost everything, God's precious face is magnificently clear.

Just as anger can keep us from being open with God, despair can inhibit the faith to seek Him. When our faith isn't strong enough to meet the need of the moment, we must pray for it. Yet it takes faith to pray for faith. That is what faith is all about. It is reaching out when we can't see. As Job said, "Yet does not one in a heap of ruins stretch out his hand, or in his disaster therefore cry out for help?" (Job 30:24) When our life is a heap of ruins, we must reach out past the rubble, where we can't see, to the merciful hand of God.

We can seek God through His Word and through fervent prayer. Another way to seek God is to look back on how He has been faithful in the past. Job spoke with fond memories of his former "days when God watched over" him (Job 29:2). God often commanded the Children of Israel to make rock piles or altars to serve as reminders of His faithfulness. When we feel our faith slipping, we can often save it by grabbing hold of memories of how God has worked in the past. This is also a good time to remember that God doesn't change.

Hushed
Job vented his soul completely during God's silence and then became silent himself. After a final plea of innocence, Job promised that his speeches were over by declaring, "Behold, here is my signature; let the Almighty answer me!" (Job 31:35) Elihu, the next speaker, gave Job several chances for rebuttals, but Job remained silent (Job 33:5; 34:33; 35:2). Silence was part of the process that Job went through in seeking God. God completed the process with His speech, but not until Job was humbly silent. Communication is two-way, but it is important to let God have the last word.

TAKING IT HOME

Choose one of the areas from the acrostic H.I.G.H. that you would like to concentrate on this week. Complete at least one assignment under that heading.

Honest

1. Read through the following list of emotions. When you see an emotion you feel, stop. Tell the Lord how you feel and why. Continue through the list. Close by thanking Him for loving you and listening to you.

angry	frustrated	safe
sad	scared	resentful
happy	proud	loving
worried	ashamed	jealous
peaceful	overwhelmed	confident
excited	weary	pleased
thankful	alone	inadequate
guilty	insecure	

2. Start a journal that is a letter to God. Start each entry with: "Dear Lord, today I feel. . . ." If you don't want to feel the way you do, pray that He will help change your heart. Go back to this journal a few weeks from now and see the answered prayers.

Immovable Faith

1. Work on getting a firm foundation of faith. Read two verses a day from the following list. Jot down their meaning. At the end of the week, write a *Statement of Faith* to keep in your Bible.

Hebrews 13:8	Matthew 28:20	2 Timothy 3:16-17
1 John 1:9	1 Corinthians 10:13	Romans 8:16-17
Hebrews 7:25	2 Corinthians 4:17	Romans 8:28
Romans 8:38-39	2 Thessalonians 3:3	Romans 10:9
Galatians 2:20	James 1:5	Ephesians 3:20-21

2. Make a list of "rock piles" in your life where God has shown His love and faithfulness to you. Share this list with a Christian friend. Another idea is to display pictures or knickknacks that remind you of events where God worked in your life.

God Seeking
1. Start a prayer journal. Keep track of your prayers of worship and praise. Speak to God of your longings. Write also about requests that you make to God. If God grants a request, mark your calendar with a symbol of your thanks.
2. Obtain several records or tapes with Christian music that use Scripture. Saturate your spirit with God's Word by listening to the music as much as possible. When you can't be listening, try to keep a song on your mind.

Hushed
Have a time each day of complete prayer. A possible format is A.C.T.S. (Adoration, Confession, Thanksgiving, Supplication). As part of your supplication (or requests), ask God to speak to you on an issue. Remain silent for a while. Keep your mind quiet; don't be planning or thinking of something else. If Scriptures come to mind, use a concordance and look them up. Thank God for speaking to you through His Word.

REFINEMENT

The following are suggestions for prayer:
1. Pray that God will strengthen your faith. Ask Him to make His presence obvious to you.
2. Have a time of confession to the Lord. Confess your sins. Next, open your feelings to Him.
3. Ask God to reveal to you what area of your faith needs bolstering. Read one of the Scriptures under that heading as prayers.

HONEST	IMMOVABLE FAITH
Psalm 55:1-8	Psalm 28:6-9
Psalm 39	Habakkuk 3:16-19
Psalm 139:23-24	Lamentations 3:19-24

GOD SEEKING	HUSHED
Psalm 27:4-8	Psalm 62:5-8, 11-12
Psalm 63:1-8	Psalm 131

4. Read Colossians 1:9-14. Pray a similar prayer for a friend.

5

SERVING THE SUFFERER

SIFTING FOR NUGGETS

1. Read Job 2:11-13. What initial steps did Job's three friends take to comfort him?

2. Eliphaz, the leader of the group, was the first speaker after Job's opening lament. Read Job 4:1-9. What point was Eliphaz making to Job?

3. Eliphaz's speech began three cycles of debate over Job's integrity. In the debate, harsh words flowed between Job and his friends. Read the following passages and write, in your own words, the harmful statements that each friend made.

   Eliphaz: Job 15:1-13

   Bildad: Job 8:1-7

   Zophar: Job 11:1-6, 13-16

4. What accusations did Job make against his friends?

   Job 13:4

Job 19:2-3

Job 21:34

5. What are some subtle ways that we mock or insult hurting friends if we aren't careful?

6. What dangers come from giving wrong answers to spiritual questions that our friends ask?

7. One way that we take the chance of giving wrong answers is to attempt to speak for God. Read the following verses. What were some of the promises that Job's friends made for God?

Job 8:20-22

Job 11:13-19

Job 22:21-23

8. Read the following statements that Job made. (Some of his words are sarcastic.) What impact did the advice of Job's friends have on him? (Job 12:1-4; 19:1-6; 26:1-3)

9. In Job 15:11-13 and 18:1-4, the friends showed that they were aware of Job's anger, yet they continued to goad him. What would be a better way to respond to a friend who felt Job's kind of anger?

10. Read Job 13:3-5 and 13 for Job's perspective of his friends' words. What are the dangers of speaking too much, even if we say the right thing?

11. Read Job 6:14. Do you think that a Christian can affect a friend's spiritual condition? If so, how?

12. Job longed for kind deeds from his friends. Read the following verses and see if you can think of some practical help that someone could have given Job.

    ❦ Job 7:5

    ❦ Job 13:5-6

    ❦ Job 17:6

    ❦ Job 19:16

    ❦ Job 30:30

13. Think of a time when your own life was particularly difficult. Did anyone perform acts of service that helped you? What were they?

14. In Job 16:4-5, Job said that our mouths can strengthen those in pain. Read Ephesians 4:29. Can you think of words friends have spoken to you that built you up in a time of need? What were they?

15. Reflect for a moment on the experience of Job and his "helping" friends. In view of this, what attitudes, words, or actions would you recommend to someone who wanted to be of genuine help to a person in pain?

STAKING A CLAIM

It was 8:00 in the morning. The piercing pain in my head coupled with dizziness made me nauseated. It had been this way for months. Now even my marriage seemed in serious trouble. The talk yesterday with Ellen had helped, but I still had to face today.

I answered the knock at the door. I knew it would be Ellen. We both cried as she hugged me.

"When I was praying for you last night, I told God how mad I was," she said.

"I think I'm mad at God."

"He can handle that. We'll keep praying," she said. "I keep thinking that He must have big plans for you someday."

She washed my dishes and dressed my two-year-old twins. When she left, I knew she would be back. Half an hour from her busy schedule had made a big difference in my day.

Job didn't have even one faithful friend. He had no one to encourage or serve him. He said, "I have become a brother to jackals, and a companion of ostriches" (Job 30:29). Let's look at what jackals, ostriches, and friends really do.

Jackals use cunning to attack weak prey. They use vultures as visual aids, making them dangerous to seriously wounded animals. Job's three friends were jackals. When we studied their speeches, we read their biting words. Their holy attitude and horrid actions caused serious damage. By claiming to be God's emissaries and acting like Job's adversaries, they helped Job put God in the jackal category too. In chapter 16, Job combined the image of God with his jackal friends by stating:

> His anger has torn me and hunted me down,
> He has gnashed at me with His teeth;
> My adversary glares at me.
> They have gaped at me with their mouth,
> They have slapped me on the cheek with contempt.
> —Job 16:9-10

Job must have felt close to those he called jackals, for he also called them brothers. We often feel freer to say harsh words to those with whom we are intimate. When we first meet someone, we put our best foot forward; with time and intimacy, we put it in our mouth. The

43

deeper the relationship, the deeper the pain we can cause. When hearts are open, consider each move as delicate surgery.

Ostriches are famous for "burying their heads in the sand." As popular myth tells it, ostriches foolishly believe that what they don't look at will go away. It is hard to watch a person we love suffer. We don't know what to say or do. We are afraid to make mistakes, and so we often stay away. But if we choose to bury our heads, jackals often go in our place.

Friends serve friends. Job's friends let him talk, but they did not listen. They were probably just waiting for their turn to speak.

What does listening accomplish? First, it serves the sufferer by letting her know that she is not alone. A listening ear is always attached to a warm body and this is of some comfort in itself.

Another purpose for listening is that it gives the sufferer a vent for her pain. If our friend chooses us as a vent, we must listen in an accepting manner. If we criticize her painful outcry, she will not feel release of her pent-up emotions. Instead, she may defend herself, in her injured state, with even tighter restraint. Job himself expressed this problem by saying, "If I speak, my pain is not lessened, and if I hold back, what has left me?" (Job 16:6)

Job stated that "the words of one in despair belong to the wind" (Job 6:26). When our friends are in despair, they often feel confused and angry. What they say at first reflects that inner turmoil. A good friend will let most of the initial outpouring of pain go "to the wind." In this way, talking can lessen the sufferer's pain. With time, her words will become less rash.

Someone who plans to serve a sufferer must listen to find out what her needs are. Usually, we can do nothing about the overwhelming problem, but we can ease our friend's smaller burdens. If we serve our suffering friends by taking care of other pressures such as children, housework, or meals, she can put more energy into meeting her own needs. With less pressure, she can concentrate on enduring the tragedy and seeking God. This can cause the problem to seem less overwhelming.

Sometimes, we feel our friend's pain so intensely, that we are afraid we won't be strong enough for her. This fear can make us stay away and can inhibit our ability to give comfort. Job said that if he were to switch places with his friends, the solace of his lips would lessen their pain (Job 16:5). So what would his lips say to bring comfort? Nothing. The Hebrew word for solace means to quiver or grieve. The sentence actually reads that the quivering of his lips would lessen their pain. Our lips quiver when we are about to cry. If Job's friends had been on the verge of tears, Job would have been comforted. It is not wise words that cut the pain; it is shared tea and tears.

Job said his friends were deceitful like wadis (Job 6:15-21). A wadi is a desert stream that causes flash floods but then disappears. Job said that travelers expecting the life-giving waters from wadis "were disappointed because they had trusted." To let a friend trust us to remain faithful and then to fail them is the worst type of deceit. If we promise to be there, we should.

Job made what seemed like a strange request. He asked his verbose friends to teach him (Job 6:24). They had been trying to impart their wisdom to him, so what did Job want? There are twelve Hebrew words for teach. They mean train, impart wisdom or knowledge, chasten or enlighten. The word Job chose actually means to shoot or to cast. His statement could have read "shoot me." Job was not requesting a mercy killing, but guidance. Think about what it takes to shoot an arrow. You hold it, point it in the right direction, get strength behind it, and LET GO.

When friends suffer, they may ask us what to do. We often think we have their answer. We tell them, remind them, and keep a tight hold to make sure that they don't get off course. What is needed more often is simply to be pointed in a positive direction, and to be given support. The hard part is often to let them go. Their choices are their own. We can watch and pray. If they miss the mark by our standards, it is not necessarily our place to say so. We can give comfort and support. If guidance is asked for again, we are free to try again.

It is not wisdom and answers that serve the sufferer, but love. What is important is not what we say to them, but that we stay with them. Listen and serve, give love and solace. God can do the rest!

Taking it home

Choose one or more of the following ideas to serve a sufferer this week.

1. Think of someone you know who is experiencing an emotionally difficult time. Invite her out for coffee, soda, or lunch. Arrange for

baby-sitting if it is applicable. Spend time listening as much as possible. Listen for needs. When you speak, try to affirm her.
2. Invite a single person (elderly or young) to share dinner and spend the evening with your family.
3. Think of someone who needs encouragement because she is overburdened. Make a list of possible needs you could meet for her. Call her and offer to do something specific for her.
4. Think of someone who is sick. Leave a "care basket" at her front door. Some ideas for the basket are baked goods, canned soup, specialty tea, bath oil, a book, or flowers.
5. Bring a dinner to a family who could use it.

REFINEMENT

The following are suggestions for prayer:
1. Ask the Lord to develop an awareness in you for the needs of others.
2. Pick a friend to pray for. Set aside a lengthy amount of time. Pray specifically for as many of her needs as you can think of. Thank the Lord for giving her to you as a friend. Ask Him to help you know how best to support her.
3. Read John 17:9-17. Jot down the requests Jesus made to God on behalf of His friends who were about to suffer. Pray those requests for a suffering friend.
4. Pray for courage to be with grieving friends. Pray that the Lord will prepare you to support your friends if they encounter deep loss in the future.
5. Pray for sensitivity. Ask the Lord to make you keenly aware of the feelings and areas of vulnerability of your friends. Ask Him to make you an encourager.

6

SENDING THE SUFFERER TO GOD

SIFTING FOR NUGGETS

1. Read at one sitting all of Elihu's speech in Job 32–37. What are your general impressions of the speech and the speaker?

2. Look more carefully at Job 32:1-10. What was the motivating factor that caused Elihu to speak? What kept him from speaking earlier?

3. Why was Elihu angry with Job and his friends?

4. Read Job 32:11-14. This section was directed toward the three friends. How might addressing them first help Elihu earn an audience with Job?

5. Read Job 33:1-7. This is Elihu's prologue to his speeches directed toward Job. In this section, what attitude distinguishes Elihu from the other three friends?

6. Read Job 33:8-12. Compare this passage to the statements of Job 10:7; 16:16-17; and 13:24-27. What did Elihu demonstrate to Job at the onset of his speech?

7. Compare the following statements of Elihu to the statements of the three companions. How did Elihu allow for better communication than the others?

Elihu	Friends
Job 33:5	Job 18:2
Job 33:6	Job 15:9-10
Job 33:32b	Job 11:5

8. Has there been a time when you didn't want to listen, yet someone got through to you? If so, what caused you to listen?

9. Elihu and the friends all requested that Job remain silent during their speeches. What would you be thinking while you were silently listening to the following speeches?
Zophar—Job 11:1-6

Eliphaz—Job 15:1-6

Elihu—Job 33:31-33

10. Once Elihu knew that Job was listening, he began to ask thought-provoking questions. What do you think Elihu was trying to teach Job through the following questions?
Job 34:17

Job 34:31-33

Job 35:2

Job 36:22-23

Job 36:29

11. What are some advantages of learning by answering questions rather than by being told directly?

12. Read Job 34:11, 34-37, and 37:23. Elihu seems to have fallen prey to the false doctrine of the first three friends. (See Job 4:7-9 and 11:13-19.) This caused them all, to varying extents, to view Job's situation incorrectly. Write a statement defining the false belief of all four friends concerning God and justice.

13. What advice did Elihu give Job?
    Job 35:14b

    Job 36:18

    Job 36:21

    Job 36:24

    Job 37:14

14. Mixed in with the advice in these chapters are accusations (Job 34:7-9, 34-37; 35:13-16; 36:21). Are these related to Job's sinfulness before or during the trial? How does this differ from the accusations of the friends?

15. Read Job 35:5-16. What basic view of God did Elihu try to give Job?

16. What actions on our part might lead our friends toward a larger view of God?

STAKING A CLAIM

I thought that the most exciting gift I could give our talkative twins was a pair of walkie-talkies. I found, however, that there are several problems with these toys. First, in order to listen, someone has to let go of the talk button. But neither of my children readily relinquishes the role of speaker. Second, the mechanisms themselves rarely work for any length of time.

Communication between two adults is often even less successful than talk between my twins on their walkie-talkies. It is easier to pry grubby little fingers off of a talk button than it is to get an upset adult to truly listen. So how did Elihu get Job to listen? It seems that by his actions, he demonstrated that he had a good attitude, a good approach, and good advice.

Attitude

Elihu was angry at everyone, yet he managed a controlled response. He stated, "I am full of words; the spirit within me constrains me" (Job 32:18). A good place for us to start with our friends is to be constrained by the Holy Spirit. Before a conversation even begins, it is wise to pray that the Lord will help us to control our tongues.

Elihu's opening statement demonstrated humility (Job 33:6-7), vulnerability (Job 32:6), and support (Job 32:32). God allows us to see these postures through Elihu's statements. We should be aware, however, that these attitudes are often proved or disproved before we ever open our mouths. Our actions, expressions, and body language often determine whether someone will listen to us. We can also follow Elihu's example by promising not to pressure our friend (Job 33:7).

Approach

One of the main differences between Elihu and the other friends was that Elihu listened well to Job. He was able to indirectly quote many of Job's key assertions (Job 33:8-11; 34:3-9; 35:3). Some of these were verbatim quotes from Job, while others were Elihu's amplified version. We could learn to begin similar discussions by rewording Elihu's statement from Job 33:8 to "This is what I heard you say." From here, we can follow Elihu's format for communication:

- After quoting Job, Elihu attempted to define what Job had said by asking a question (Job 33:13). This gave Job a chance to respond or clarify.
- Elihu pointed out the error in Job's thinking (Job 33:12).
- Rather than dwell on Job's sin, Elihu attempted to widen his view of God (Job 33:14-30).
- Elihu again invited Job to respond (Job 33:32).
- He reaffirmed his support for Job by saying, "I desire to justify you" (Job 33:32).

Elihu's last statement brings up an important question to ask ourselves: What are our motives for advising our friend? If we are seeking to demonstrate our wisdom, there are more prudent ways than giving advice. If we are truly seeking to justify our friend, we need only to help her go to God. Only He can bring true justification. Head to head human confrontation can obstruct the sufferer's view of God. When standing in the dark shadows of tragedy, a sufferer needs a friend beside her to help her see that God is light.

Elihu gave Job the opportunity for some deep thinking by asking thought-provoking questions. (These should be distinguished from the antagonistic questions of the friends.) In chapters 34 through 36, Elihu asked twenty-one spiritual questions. This tactic appears to be a commendable one, as it was the only method God used with Job!

Advice

Elihu's next step was to point out Job's sin. If there is any area where even angels fear to tread it is probably here. If we attempt it, we should do so with great care and much prayer. If we earn that right, it is only after applying all that we have learned thus far in this book.

Elihu was not much gentler than the friends, but the sins he pointed out were different. The three companions accused Job of prior sins that could have caused the trial. Elihu pointed out Job's sinful attitude that resulted *from* the trial. No one can go back in time and undo sins that have been committed. When trying to correct a friend, dwelling on her past errors is futile. But helping our friend develop a humble and repentant heart will heal the past and begin to set the present in order. This lesson is best taught by example. The Apostle John said, "If we confess our sins, He is faithful and righteous to forgive us our sins and to cleanse us from all unrighteousness" (1 John 1:9). The only thing that can alter the past is the altar of God.

Elihu assisted Job by helping him to see his attitude and to see how God communicated. God communicates in a much different way with us than He did with Job. Because of Jesus, the Holy Spirit can work directly within us. The Holy Spirit rarely works within us to convict someone else! We must learn to stop pointing our fingers and begin, instead, to draw our friends to God. When God has a Spirited conversation, it is much different than the ones we have!

God's main way to communicate with us is through the Bible. Hebrews 4:12 gives us the encouragement that "the Word of God is living and active," along with a warning that it is "sharper than any two-edged sword." But if we grab hold of a convicting verse and thrust it at our suffering friend, we can cause harm. How much more effective to place the sword of the Word into her own hands! We can encourage her to use it and give her some direction. We can study a subject together with her, or suggest a passage or book that has encouraged us. From here, the Holy Spirit can do the teaching.

Elihu warned Job to beware and to be careful not to sink into sin. Next, he told him to behold God's power in storms (Job 37:18-22). Throughout chapter 37, Elihu described the tempest so vividly that we can picture the scene. The cumulation of Job's stormy trial brought more than cumulus clouds. A complete storm appeared. The tension in the air became electric as lightning, and thunder struck almost simultaneously. God set the stage for His speech and Elihu excitedly finished his own. He faced the storm and saw God. Elihu announced the presence of the Lord in the clouds, thunder, lightning, and rain (Job 36:27-33; 37:6-12). He urged Job to "stand and consider the wonders of God" (Job 37:14).

In the end, God neither condemned nor commended Elihu. Some of what Elihu said was similiar to complaints of the other friends. His view was human and imperfect. We *can*, however, learn from Elihu's methods of communication and his attempt to send the sufferer to God. God excluded Elihu from His rebuke of the three friends, but Elihu could never receive credit for the spiritual healing of Job. No human help is ever completely sufficient. Only God can restore.

Elihu helped a suffering saint see the Sovereign in the storm. This must be our emphasis as well. If we can help our suffering friends see that God is with them in their storms, we will have done well. If we can help them to go to our awesome and merciful God, we will have succeeded. We need not have the answers; only God has those. Maybe we, like Elihu, will be alllowed to witness the miraculous transformation of a servant coming through refinement into godly gold.

TAKING IT HOME

1. Think of someone you know who seems to be struggling with an area of her life. Pray that the Lord would show you ways that you could begin to spend consistent time together. Think of ways that

you could earn an audience with her so that you could give encouragement and support. Ask God to show you how to demonstrate a vulnerable and loving attitude. Pray for wisdom as to know when to initiate contact. If you feel a peace, call her up this week.

2. Make a list of thought provoking-questions that could help someone to examine her relationship with God. Then answer the questions for yourself. Save your answers.
3. Get together with another member of the group and practice some role playing. Have conversations using the following format.
   1. Person A talks about a hypothetical problem that she is having.
   2. Person B listens without interrupting.
   3. Person B summarizes person A's speech and asks for clarification.
   4. Person A confirms or reclarifies.
   5. Person B asks thought-provoking spiritual questions in response to what person A has shared.
4. If you know someone who is struggling to make a decision or just needs hope, pray the prayer in Ephesians 1:15-21. Write her a note quoting the verse/prayer you are praying for her.

REFINEMENT

1. Pray that the Lord will make you a better listener.
2. If you are in a position of disciplining or counseling someone, pray for a humble attitude. Pray for a willingness to be open and vulnerable. Pray for wisdom.
3. If you know someone to whom you ought to give counsel, pray that the Holy Spirit will work mightily in both of you. Pray that He will control your desire to give unwanted advice. Pray that your friend will develop a hunger for the Lord at a new depth. Pray that she will seek counsel from you or from someone else who can lead her to a deeper knowledge of the Lord.
4. Pray that the Lord will broaden your view of Him. Pray that you can use that broadened view for His glory.

7

SAVIOR'S ANSWERS

Sifting for Nuggets

1. Read Job 38:1-2. What was God's initial accusation to Job?

2. Read Romans 1:20. What is God's creation meant to demonstrate?

3. Job had darkened God's counsel (or teaching) by using examples from creation to illustrate his own doubts and questions. He used his limited view of the world to make broad questions about what God does and values. Read what Job was able to see—and not see.

Example	Question
Land formations (Job 14:18-22)	Does God destroy hope?
Ox and wild donkey (Job 24:1-5)	Does God cause oppression?

The Lord responded to Job with enlightenment, not punishment. God wanted Job to know the truth. God used Job's own examples to show His original intent at creation. What does each example show about what God's values?

Example	Value of God
Land formation (Job 38:4-7)	
Ox/donkey (Job 39:5-10)	

How do God's teachings here illumine Job's limited view?

4. The cycles of nature raised more questions about God in Job's mind.

Example	Question
Light/darkness (Job 19:7-8)	Does God use darkness to confuse us?
Storms (Job 30:21-23)	Does God use His power to hurt us?

God said that He uses these cycles to accomplish good.

Example	What God does through it
Light/darkness (Job 38:12-15)	
Storms (Job 38:25-27)	

5. Job saw the world through the viewpoint of his own seemingly hopeless situation. Job wondered if members of the animal kingdom illustrated his own plight.

Example	Plight
Eagle (Job 9:25-26)	Does God care that my life is slipping away?
Lion (Job 10:16)	Must I cower before God?
Ostrich (Job 30:28-29)	Does God treat His people as mere animals?

God's speech showed that He sees the world through the perspective of each creature. He showed His ability to care for His creatures under perilous conditions. What must God do to keep the young offspring of the following species alive? What is demonstrated about God's ability to sustain His creatures?

Example	Ability of God
Eagle (Job 39:27-30)	
Lion (Job 38:39-40)	
Ostrich (Job 39:13-15)	

6. When has some aspect of God's creation raised questions about His character in your own mind?

How has God's creation helped you to know Him better?

7. God's first speech (chapters 38–39), gave Job a wide view of creation. In God's second speech (chapters 40–41), He concentrated on two animals: the Behemoth (Job 40:15-24), and the leviathon (Job 41:1-34). Scholars differ on what these two creatures actually were and thus they remain two of God's mysteries. Whatever they were, God used them to make a point. Read the opening statements of this speech in Job 40:6-14. What was to be God's topic of discussion?

8. What circumstances in your life have caused you to wonder about God's justice, His kindness, or His power?

9. The words from God's speech may not sound very tender. He never answered the majority of Job's questions. God never explained the reason for the trial nor did He reveal to Job the throne room scene with Satan. Instead, God offered His own presence. Read Psalm 16:7-11 and list some of the benefits of being in God's presence.

10. Read the following verses and fill in the chart. What were the things that Job cried out to God for? In what ways does Christ answer those same cries of mankind today?

Job's Cries	Christ's Answers
Job 7:21	Acts 10:43
Job 9:33-34	1 Timothy 2:5-6
Job 14:14	John 3:16
Job 16:19-21	1 John 2:1
Job 19:25-27	Colossians 1:13-19
Job 23:3	John 14:5-7

11. Elihu felt that he knew what an angel would do to solve Job's problem. He described this heavenly mediator in Job 33:23-28. Read that passage and Paul's description of Christ's role in 1 Timothy 2:3-6. Write down what the two passages have in common.

12. Has Jesus answered some of your own cries of pain? If so, how?

13. When you suffer, what is it (besides changed circumstances) that you want from God? Has He promised to do that? Use a concordance, a friend, or a pastor to help you find the answer.

STAKING A CLAIM

It was Passover week, a week for Jews to celebrate their deliverance from oppression. Yet first-century Israel groaned beneath the weight of Roman rule. God's people were burdened with unexpressed questions about their unexplainable quandary. Where was God? Why didn't He save them? What had happened to His faithfulness?

God had already sent His answer, but few recognized it. A small crowd gathered around a cross. The day turned dark and stormy. God responded in an astonishing way to the questions and pain of His people: His only Son died in agony for them.

Our creative Creator often answers in surprising ways. At the end of the Book of Job, a small crowd gathered around an agonized man. The day turned stormy. Job felt that God owed him an explanation for his suffering. He called the Judge to justify Himself, and the Sovereign answered the subpoena. But the trial took an unforeseen course. God entered the courtroom in a whirlwind and interrogated Job!

God asked Job over seventy unanswerable questions. In God's first speech, He gave a panoramic view of nature. In His second speech, He challenged Job to try to act as supreme administrator of justice. God did not justify Himself. Instead He caused Job to see His own wrong in questioning God's judgment.

God's responses to us are often not what we expect. He works on the basis of eternal purpose rather than on immediate problems. Our life on earth is but a speck of our own eternal spectrum. Our primary need is to be one with God for eternity. God became man to meet that need. As a result, man can come to God with any need. We will study how Jesus responds to us as we look at the acrostic J.E.S.U.S.

Joins us
Empathizes with us
Soothes and comforts us
Understands our weaknesses
Supplicates (prays) for us

Joins Us

The Book of Matthew demonstrates how Jesus joined mankind from conception through resurrection. Chapter 1 explains that while Mary was still pregnant, an angel announced that Immanuel means "God with us" (Matthew 1:23). Matthew chronicles Christ's loving interactions with people during His ministry. The last verse of the book shows His final statement, "Lo, I am with you always, even to the end of the age" (Matthew 28:20).

Christ's promise applies to us today. He is with us. However dark our circumstances may seem, the Light of the world is with us (John 8:12). However alone we may feel, His presence is constant. No matter how deep our grief, this man of sorrows bears it with us (Isaiah 53:3-5).

Empathizes with Us

Jesus is not an unfeeling lord who sits up in heaven wondering why we cry so much. His soul has been "deeply grieved, to the point of death" (Matthew 26:38). He too has prayed with "loud crying and tears" (Hebrews 5:7).

As women, we may feel that Jesus can't fully empathize with us. Jesus was never a woman, yet He experienced many of the sorrows and frustrations common to women. He was never a woman working in a man's world, but He was a Jew working in a Roman world. Jesus never went through childbirth, yet He suffered excruciating pain on the cross to give us spiritual birth. He never raised a house full of children. Instead, He became caretaker for twelve bickering disciples. He met their needs twenty-four hours a day. He faced constant demands of crowds and didn't have anyone around who could speak at His level. That sounds like motherhood!

During the last week of His life, Jesus experienced many of the abuses women sometimes suffer at the hands of men. He was betrayed, abandoned, and ridiculed. He was physically abused. Before the Crucifixion, He was publicly stripped, struck repeatedly in the face, and whipped (Matthew 27:27-31).

Jesus never experienced a divorce, but He knows the pain. He knows the ache of feeling betrayed by a loved one (Matthew 26:47-50). Divorce is so devastating because it is the tearing apart of two who were once one. Jesus was one with the Father (John 10:30), yet on the cross, God turned His back on Him. When Jesus cried, "My God, My God, why hast Thou forsaken Me?" (Matthew 27:46), He knew the pain of a torn heart. No matter what our situation, Jesus can empathize with us.

Soothes and Comforts

Jesus suffered so that He can be our perfect comforter (2 Corinthians 1:5). Our aching hearts can climb into His spiritual lap to sob with Him. We can cry out, "It hurts so badly!" He silently responds that He knows how much it hurts because He is feeling it too.

Christ's presence can soothe our aching hearts. A sudden remembering that He loves us can comfort our souls. A flood of peace, while spending time in His Word, is supernatural solace. Knowing that He is in control is rest for our tormented minds. Jesus is not only the Savior of our souls, but also our anchor in times of suffering.

Understands
Satan knows that testing brings temptation. This is why he tested Job. Jesus also knows the temptations we face in times of suffering. He not only knows, he understands.

> For we do not have a high priest who cannot sympathize with our weaknesses, but one who has been tempted in all things as *we are, yet* without sin. Let us therefore draw near with confidence to the throne of grace, that we may receive mercy and may find grace to help in time of need (Hebrews 4:15-16).

Our most dangerous temptation, when we are hurt, is to hide from the Lord. He will not scold us for feeling angry and wanting to lash out. Jesus will not chide us for being tempted to run away or hide from our problems. We must go to Him while these *feelings* are still just temptations. He does not say, "I didn't sin; what's your problem?" Instead, His response to us is "I know how hard it is to obey when everything seems horrible. Come, let Me help you!"

Supplicates
Job realized that to present a case to God without help would be futile. He said that he needed an advocate to speak for him (Job 16:19-21). Now we can know that Jesus is our advocate as He supplicates for us. He intercedes for us at the right hand of God (Romans 8:34). If we become the subject of a throne room discussion like Job did, Jesus Himself will speak for us. Who could add to that kind of supplication?

The earthly answers we find in our trials are not of primary importance. As long as we respond to Jesus, God responds to us through Jesus. He is our only answer.

As I look back on my life, I can see that Jesus has been exactly what I have needed in trials. One night, near the end of a wearying ordeal, I sketched this poem. I was seeing that my Savior was my answer.

I lay awake recalling trials
That had bombarded me
The water I'd been dropped into
A wicked perilous sea
I was angry

I fought the turbid deep
'Til I thought my lungs would burst
Lost hope of God's deliverance
"He's here but gives the worst"
I was untrusting

Then raging storms did cease
I cried, "I've passed the test
My enemy was less than I
I know I did my best"
I was proud

My wounded heart I salved
Sitting safely on the shore
Clutching tight what I had left
I said, "No Lord, no more"
I was rebellious

You gently spoke to me
And pointed out my sin
You took my wounded heart in Yours
My pain You felt within
I was healed

Taking it home

1. Make a list of some of your favorite aspects of God's creation. Think of what each one demonstrates about the goodness of God. Share your thoughts with a friend or family member.
2. Next time you feel really depressed, have a good cry with Jesus. Allow Him to comfort you. Try to visualize His strong, gentle arms cradling you as you cry.

3. Think through the events of Christ's life and meditate on His sufferings. Try to empathize with the pain He felt. Think of ways that His sufferings are similar to some of yours. Thank Jesus for living and dying and empathizing with you.
4. Pick one day this week to be especially aware of the Lord's presence. As you go through the day, remind yourself that He is with you. Each time you feel frustrated, sad, joyful, weary, or worried, thank Him for being with you.

REFINEMENT

1. Many scholars believe that Psalm 22 is a prophetic psalm about Jesus. Read Psalm 22:1-19. Try to imagine Jesus praying this prayer on the cross. Note the cries of agony interlaced with praise. Notice statements of trust in the midst of pain. Observe the pleas for God to be near to Him. Now pray your own prayer to the Lord. Try to include the aspects of prayer found in Psalm 22. Thank Jesus for going through so much agony for you.
2. Ask Jesus to let you be extremely aware of His presence. Pray that you will identify your pain with His. Ask Him to make His comfort known to you in a deep and obvious way.
3. Pray for a suffering friend. Ask that Jesus will comfort her. Pray that she will be very aware of Jesus' presence.
4. Read 2 Corinthians 1:3-4. Pray that Jesus will teach you to be a comforter to others.

8

SURVIVORS

SIFTING FOR NUGGETS

1. Read Job's response to God's first speech (Job 40:3-5). In as few words as possible, restate what Job said.

2. God's second speech brought a more complete response from Job. Read Job 42:1-6. Fill in the spiritual steps that Job took in his reaction to God's second speech.

   Job 42:2
   Job 42:3a (quoted God from Job 38:2)
   Job 42:3b
   Job 42:4 (quoted God from Job 38:3)
   Job 42:5
   Job 42:6a
   Job 42:6b

3. Throughout the Book of Job, Job begged God to meet with him. What did Job gain from his audience with God?

4. When God finished speaking, Job repented. Why?

5. When has your own experience with God changed you in some significant way?

6. Read Job 42:7-9. What phrase did God repeat when He spoke to Job's friends?

7. Why do you think God made the friends bring the sacrifice to Job?

8. Job repented. His trial ended. He survived. Yet God still required much of him. Job had to act as priest to those who had hurt him. Write down what work was required of Job in the following areas:
   Physical work

   Emotional work

   Spiritual work

9. What was required of the three friends in order to reconcile with Job and with God?

10. Read Job 42:10-17. What gifts did God give to Job? (Find all that you can.)

11. Read Job 19:13-19. Now read Job 42:10-11. Job was probably talking about the same people in both passages. If you were Job, which would have been harder for you, to feed these people or to accept their gifts? Why?

12. Review Job 2:9-10 and 19:17. What do you think it took to restore the relationship between Job and his wife?

13. Have you ever felt that you ought to forgive someone and found it difficult? What has helped you to be able to offer the gift of forgiveness?

14. Job was a righteous man, yet he lost all that he had—and God didn't even tell him why. One major lesson throughout the Book of Job is that there is no direct relationship between doing good and material reward. God does not *owe* us anything. Why then do you think that the book ends with Job being happy and prosperous?

15. Do you think that Job still grieved for what he had lost? Explain.

16. Think back to when you started this study. List blessings you have received since that time. Include gifts from God, spiritual growth, and material blessings.

17. Thank God for these expressions of His kindness.

STAKING A CLAIM

October 17, 1989 was a memorable day for northern Californians. The actual earthquake lasted minutes, yet the entire earth-shattering experience lingered for months. My parents' three-story house was severely damaged. For them, terms such as split-level homes, open-beam ceilings, and detached garages took on new meaning.

My family survived the earthquake but was left with an enormous amount of work. There were truckloads of debris to be removed. Walls, floors, and roofs needed to be rebuilt. With no electricity, this would have been an insurmountable task. But my father was farsighted enough to own a generator. Within hours, he had lights glowing and power tools buzzing. With the skill and muscle of family and friends, work began immediately.

Trials often become like earthquakes. Even when the traumatic experience is over, the work is yet to be done. Lives need to be repaired. Relationships need to be put back on their foundations. Hurt feelings and emotional debris must be dealt with. These tasks will be insurmountable if we are not plugged into the only true power source: God.

For Job, the whirlwind signaled the end of his series of supernatural disasters. He had survived the onslaught, and Satan was defeated. But new wealth and children would not have restored Job. Curing his disease would not have healed his heart. A wounded man still struggled beneath a pile of emotional and spiritual rubble. The Lord had a blueprint for Job to follow to reconstruct his life. It involved repentance, renewal with God, and reconciliation with others. Then God, in His infinite love, chose to bring Job to restored joy.

Repentance
God's accusations to Job were that he had spoken beyond his knowledge (Job 38:1-2), and that he had tried to reprove God (Job 40:1-2). Job had crossed a fine line between venting his anger and accusing God of wrongdoing. To try to find fault in our searingly holy God is not only futile, but sinful. When we are unhappy with the actions of the Sovereign, a respectful appeal beats a rude approach.

I have often had to confess my anger toward God. My sin is not the prayers in which I have poured out my feelings to Him. What I must confess is the thought, often unexpressed, that God has wronged me. God is perfect and loving, but beyond our comprehension. When we play faultfinder with God, we ourselves are at fault. This is what we must confess.

Job's initial choice of how to deal with his presumption was incorrect. He thought that discontinuing his negative statements would solve the problem (Job 40:3-5). God wanted more from Job, not as punishment, but because He loved Job. What both of them wanted was restored fellowship. Job needed what all humans need in order to experience the joy of God's presence; he needed to repent.

God's second speech brought Job to true repentance. First, Job acknowledged God for who He is (Job 42:1-2). Next, he agreed with God's assessment of his sin (Job 42:3). This is what confession is all about. Job's final step was to repent (Job 42:6), or turn away from his sin. From this point on, he would act differently.

If Job stood in need of confession, his friends would have to follow a similar course. They had acted in arrogance. They had spoken wrongly of God. These were sins against the Lord. They had also thrown sparks of accusation into the ash pile of Job's pain. They had hurled stumbling blocks into the rubble of Job's crumbled world. These were sins against Job. God's stormy splendor doesn't seem to have melted their hearts as it had Job's. The sparks of accusation were now justifiably thrown their way in a fiery rebuke from the Lord. Their prideful hearts may have been momentarily incredulous that they were admonished and Job extolled. But as God repeated His statement, His verdict was beyond question. He found the friends guilty of sin against God and man. The Righteous Judge required them to pay their sacrifice to God through Job as a priest.

Whether we are confessing an inadequate view of God or blatant sins, we all need to repent. And as we repent, we can look to Job's example of a yearning, yielding heart. The New Testament assures us that God has already offered us forgiveness through the sacrifice of His Son. He eagerly awaits our restored fellowship.

Renewal

Job's dialogue with God led him to a complete renewal of his faith. God lifted the weight of his sin. God gave him complete forgiveness. God removed his spiritual blinders. God no longer called him the faultfinder, but His servant. Job's faith became tangible. He reveled in the revelation of the Lord (Job 42:5).

Reconciliation

The first step in reconciling relationships is a willingness to forgive. If we have been wounded and undeservedly reviled, forgiveness must take an enormous leap. God knew Job's heart. He knew that Job would accept his friends, that Job would even pray that his friends wouldn't get what they deserved. Could God make that assumption for us?

Job was ready to forgive. Nothing had yet changed in his circumstances. The friends were no different. The only new variable in the equation was Job's relationship with God. In Luke 7:47, Jesus pointed out a connection between love and forgiveness. Job is a good example of how forgiveness from God can lead to a love of others who need forgiveness.

God can give us strength to do the seemingly impossible (Philippians 4:13). It would seem impossible for a convalescing old man to do the work of sacrificing seven huge bulls and seven hefty rams!

We have our own impossibilities. For us, the impossible probably wouldn't be the preparation of animal bodies. It may be the preparation of our own hearts for the sacrifice of granting forgiveness. My experience has been that forgiveness must often be a step of obedience and the dragging along of a reluctant heart. We don't know how

Job felt about his friends' sacrifice. God did not tell Eliphaz to go to "My cheerful friend," or to "your loving brother Job." He said, "Go to My servant Job." God depended on Job's obedience.

God did not allow the friends to slink away and deny their harmful words. He did not allow wounds to fester. He did not require Job to forget the incident. He had the group face the facts and fillet their sins on the altar. These, he burned away to be seen no more. Facing hurled words facilitates healed wounds. All that was said was remembered, or we would not be able to read it today. But surely, the words were retained without grudge. The event and the book led to the glory of God.

With God's help, Job switched from hostility to hospitality. All the relatives who had shunned him came to HIS house for a feast! The exchange of food and gifts pictures restored relationships. It must have taken a lot of work for Job and his wife, but the hospitality demonstrated forgiveness. They did not stop here as the benevolent heroes who stopped to help the villains. They accepted the gifts. This brought the relationships back to mutuality.

It is often hard to accept kindness from someone who has wronged us. We must drop our pride in order to let the offender become the offerer. Only true forgiveness and the grace of God enables us to do this.

God's methods of relating to Job show His tender love for His servant. He pointed out Job's error in an array of majesty. (With the friends, however, God gave a direct angry rebuke.) God asked Job questions, knowing that Job would come to the appropriate conclusion: God is sovereign. God did not require a sacrifice from Job; neither punishment nor payment was necessary. These interactions demonstrate God's character. God facilitates the growth of His children by the flow of His grace to them. Unrepented sin would have left Job with the weight of guilt. Unforgiveness toward the friends could have left Job with shackles of bitterness. But God helped Job's heart to be free to experience restored joy. This joy was not owed, but bestowed.

Restored Joy

The human desire after a great loss is to go back in time. God's humane response is to bring us forward into new joy. God does not necessarily give back what we lost; He tends to give us new avenues of happiness. It is the joy that is restored, not the loss. This is sovereign love. God did not replace Job's former family. Job would always carry that pain. (For this, God offered the comfort of His presence and the consolation of friends and family.) But God did offer the gifts of health and new wealth. He bestowed the blessings of another family. Each of these gifts from God came individually and in His time.

Imagine the scenario. Cousin Micah comes with a coin and a ring. A little while later, Aunt Sarah does the same. Then brother Uzal, and sister Sheba, and cousin Abimael. . . . A few months later, Job's aged wife seems to feel tired and nauseous.

"Honey, you're not going to believe this, but I think I'm pregnant."

"I believe it. All the sheep and camels are pregnant too!"

Years go by and old gray-haired Mrs. Job keeps having babies and the herds keep increasing. This probably took at least twenty years. During this era, there were stabs of painful memories, but increasing times of joy.

We see over 140 years in the eight verses of Job 42:10-17. For Job, it was most of a lifetime. For God, it was the fulfillment of a decision made during ONE of Job's prayers! "And the Lord restored the fortunes of Job when he prayed for his friends" (Job 42:10).

It is easy for us to forget to give God credit for blessings that take a long time to be fulfilled. We forget the prayers we prayed years ago so that we don't recognize God's answers. God sets events into motion and accomplishes miracles, but we fail to notice.

Part of Job's restored joy was his restored perception of his worth. Job's worth came under question by those friends who believed the false doctrine of cause and effect between God and man. But the final scene must have caused these men to pause and reflect on their beliefs. God's declaration of high regard for Job validated the truth of his worth. Job's value was never diminished in God's eyes; it was merely dimmed through the human eyes of those who could not properly see.

As Christians, our worth is never threatened. Christ died for us while we were sinners (Romans 5:8), and His love for us is everlasting (Jeremiah 31:3). Regardless of what others say, the Lord holds us in high regard. No matter what we think of ourselves, we are precious children of God through faith (Galatians 3:26). Who are we to argue with God?

We all suffer fiery ordeals. We find ourselves, like Job, sitting in the ashes of what we thought was to be. If we cling to our faith, we can say as Job did: "When He has tried me I shall come forth as gold" (Job 23:10). As God looks at our ash pile, let's hope that He sees a soft, golden heart reflecting back His love. This is of great worth. Nothing melts the heart of our Daddy-God more than gold in the ashes.

TAKING IT HOME

Choose one or more of the following ideas to renew or reconcile a relationship this week.

1. Think through the people in your life to see if you owe an apology to anyone. If so, apologize to that person this week.

2. Find a way to spend an hour or two alone with God. Make this a priority, even if you have to get a baby-sitter or leave work undone. Start with a time of confession. Have a time of praising Him for who He is. Sing to Him. Thank Him for the blessings He has given you. Try some of the prayer suggestions in *Refinement*.

3. Think of someone with whom you would like to renew a relationship. Pray for ideas that you could use to accomplish this. Make contact with that person this week.

4. If you have a broken relationship because of past hurts, begin to pray for that relationship. Pray that the Lord will work in both of your hearts. If your heart needs to change to be able to forgive, pray for that change. Pray daily until you feel God's grace in you to love that person again. Pray that God will help you to accept whatever response the other person may give back to you. Pray for wisdom to know when or how to initiate reconciliation.

5. If you have been going through a trial and others have helped, write some thank-you notes this week.

6. If you and your husband have been experiencing a trial together, spend some time trying to see it from his perspective. Think of what needs he may have due to the trial. Think of needs you could meet. See if there is some reconciling that needs to be done between the two of you. Pray about this and initiate reconciliation.

7. Do a "thank-you check" with the Lord. Think back on prayers you have prayed during the past several years. Take note of requests that God has granted. If you kept prayer journals, look over

some from years past. Praise God for nurturing your spiritual growth. Thank Him for answering your prayers.

REFINEMENT

The following are suggestions for prayer:

1. If you are in the midst of a trial or have recently survived one, have a time of soul-searching. Ask the Lord if there are sins that you now need to confess. Use Psalm 139:23-24 as a prayer model.
2. If you feel that you need a time of confession, do so. Pray Psalm 51:1-17 as a pattern.
3. If you have been hurt by someone, and it is still unresolved, pray the prayer of David from Psalm 55:1-4, 12-14. Next, pray Psalm 139:23-24.
4. If you have just gone through a time of confession and renewal, pray either Psalm 30 or Psalm 32.
5. If the Lord has richly blessed you after a period of trials, pray Psalm 116.

INTRODUCTION

Guidelines for Your First Meeting

Do you want to study *Gold in the Ashes* with a group? This group study guide will give you specific suggestions to facilitate each group meeting. If group members are not acquainted with each other, try to hold a preliminary meeting before you discuss chapter 1. This preliminary meeting will help people to get acquainted with each other, receive books, learn the procedure for personal study, and allow the intervening days for personal preparation necessary to discuss chapter 1 at the next session. The following format for this introductory meeting may help:

1. As people arrive, make introductions and serve light refreshments.
2. When everyone is present, help them to get acquainted by asking some of the following questions:
   - If you had a day entirely free of responsibilities, what would you do with it?
   - Who are the members of your family?
   - What is a favorite childhood memory?
   - What was the most favorite job of your life? The least favorite?
   - What is a favorite book you've recently read?
   - If you had a thousand dollars to spend on a vacation, what would you do?
   - On a scale of 1 to 10, with 10 being high, how would you rate your current relationship with God? Explain.
   - All of us experience spiritual, physical, and emotional pain. What has been one of the "pains" in your life?

❧ Why are you interested in studying the Book of Job?

3. Introduce the Book of Job by giving brief background information. Use information from standard reference works like *The New Bible Commentary*, by D. Guthrie, A.M. Stibbs, and D.J. Wiseman, published by Eerdmans in Grand Rapids, Michigan in 1970 or *The Zondervan Pictorial Encyclopedia of the Bible*, by Merrill C. Tenney, published by Zondervan in Grand Rapids in 1976. You will also find most information that you need in any current study Bible.

4. Hand out copies of *Gold in the Ashes*. Explain that the book is designed for each member to use the front section of the book to study individually at home. Then you will use questions in the back section at group meetings to discuss your findings and explore further ways to nurture spiritual growth. Since the quality of personal growth and the quality of discussion depend on this individual study, encourage them to do the lesson.

5. Familiarize them with the format of *Gold in the Ashes*. You can use the introduction on pages 7 and 8 to help you. Point out the chart outlining the Book of Job on page 9.

6. Close in prayer.

GUIDELINES FOR WEEKLY PREPARATION

1. Pray for guidance from the Holy Spirit as you prepare to lead the study. Ask for wisdom and sensitivity.

2. Read all of the passages and make notes throughout the lesson.

3. Read the Group Study Guide and work through the steps of Leader Preparation.

4. Become familiar with the lesson. Think through the potential flow of discussion. Think of how each person in your group is likely to approach each question or activity. Consider ways to help group members interact with each other in a way that lets them benefit from each other's strengths and shore up each other's weaknesses.

5. Plan how you will cover the entire study by marking where you should be in the series of questions at various points in your hour together. Mark a few questions that you could summarize if time is short or add if you have extra time.

6. Make note of any background information or references to the main portions of the book that you want to draw into the discussion.

7. Pray, by name, for each person in the group.

GUIDELINES FOR WEEKLY SESSIONS

1. Start and end on time. Many people consider their time as valuable as their money. If you run over the time they have allowed, they will feel as robbed as if you had picked their pockets.

2. Open and close in prayer.

3. Assume that all of the group discussion questions have multiple answers. After you have asked the question, aim for a pattern of conversation that travels back and forth throughout the group. Help group members to focus on each other and on the issues and texts at hand, not on you as leader. If discussion lags and you feel that they have not yet totally answered the question, ask: "Does anyone see it a different way?" "Have we left out anything that you noticed in your own study?" When discussion seems complete, move quickly to the next question so that people do not feel a sense of lagged time.

4. Give encouraging comments. If an answer is partially correct, acknowledge that part. If an answer seems inappropriate, say something like, "What verse led you to that conclusion?" or "What do the rest of you think?"

5. Keep the discussion on track. You might want to write the objective from the group guide on a card each week. Put the card where you can see it during the meeting to remind you of what you are trying to accomplish. Don't be afraid to head off a tangent by gently continuing with your planned discussion. But do consider the tangent's merit for the group as a whole. Sometimes apparent tangents represent real needs that the group ought to address. In that case, adjust your lesson plan in stride and follow (for the moment) the needs and interests of the group. If the tangent seems of limited interest or importance, offer to talk about it in more detail at a later time. Or if the tangent is of great importance, but requires further preparation, ask the group to table it for this session but come back to it in a later meeting.

6. Encourage people to participate more or less evenly. Be on the alert for indications that shy members are ready to venture into a discussion, and draw them in. If someone speaks too often or too long, redirect the conversation toward another person. Help group members to adopt balanced participation as one of their own values. Then encourage self-discipline as each person considers her own natural bent and adjusts more toward the average. In some cases, you may need to speak privately to a person who is

too talkative or someone who never speaks at all. Be sensitive and tactful. Remember, you are the moderator of the group, not the owner. The group exists for the benefit of the people in it.

7. Don't be afraid of silence. People do great thinking during those times. Help group members to feel comfortable with silence by making a comment that allows them quiet thinking time. Then show respect for the reflections that are voiced after that period.

8. Don't worry about questions that you cannot answer. The Book of Job probably raises more unanswerable questions than any other book of Scripture. To try to answer every question raised by the Book of Job is an insult to the intelligence of the people present and an embarrassment to your own presumption. You can redirect some questions to the group. You may also say that you don't know an answer and offer to research the issue, or ask another group member to research it. You may also encourage people to live in faith, even in the face of unanswered questions. Job did.

ONE LAST THOUGHT

Because of the subject of this study, you may encounter women in great pain. Devote yourself to prayer; pray continually for the people of your group. Ask the Lord to give you sensitivity and wisdom so that you will know whom He would have you reach out to and in what way. You may want to read chapters 5 and 6 of *Gold in the Ashes* before you start the study. This will help equip you to serve a suffering friend with some degree of confidence.

But take stock of your own limitations. Many people in pain need professional help to resolve the emotional fall-out of the hurt that has pervaded their lives. Keep a list of capable counselors in your area to whom you can refer people who need their services. May the Lord use you mightily in His work!

Group Study 1

SATAN'S BATTLE, GOD'S WAR

OBJECTIVE

To help group members develop an awareness of the spiritual battle in which they are involved.

LEADER PREPARATION

🌣 Complete the *Sifting for Nuggets* section for chapter 1.

🌣 Read *Staking a Claim*.

🌣 Think of someone who is your Christian role model. Think of what types of trials this person has experienced and how those trials have affected her.

GROUP TIME

1. Who is one of your present day-heroes of faith?
   How easy or difficult has that person's life been? Explain.
2. Read Job 1:1–2:13. Describe Job in your own terms.
3. Job loved his children deeply and went to great pains to bring them to God. Describe how someone you know has shown that type of love.
4. How did Job's messengers coming in rapid succession work in Satan's favor?
5. We often say, "When it rains it pours." We all go through times when it feels like our world is crumbling. These are acute trials. How did Job respond to the acute trial described in chapter 1?
6. How do you respond when you receive an abundance of rapid-fire trials?
7. Look again at Job 1:20 and Job 2:12. If you were extremely upset or sorrowful, and no one was watching, how might you creatively express and release your feelings?
8. Why do you think that our culture doesn't include these ways of expressing emotions?
9. According to Job 2:1-3, God was satisfied with Job's performance in the first battle. What was Satan's way of subtly discounting Job's victory? (See Job 1:9-11 and 2:4-5.)
10. Look at Hebrews 8:1-2. In view of Christ's position described here, what part do you think He takes in any current throne room discussions?

11. Review your two charts on pages 12 and 13. What connections do you see between Job's trials and your own?
12. Survey again Job's response thus far to the tragedy that has plagued him. What do you hope will be a part of your own response the next time you face trial?
13. None of us can expect a life free of hardship. What are some steps that you can take now to prepare yourself for your own next period of suffering?

Group Study 2

SEARCHING FOR REASONS

OBJECTIVE
To encourage group members to have an attitude of cooperation with God rather than a habit of asking why.

LEADER PREPARATION
- Complete the *Sifting for Nuggets* section.
- Read the *Staking a Claim* section.
- Do at least one suggestion from the *Taking It Home* section.
- Contact a member of the group (preferably a mother with a sense of humor). Work with her to create a skit involving a mother and small child in a series of questions where the child asks why, the answer begets another why, and that answer begets another why. . . .
- On a large piece of paper, copy the chart from question 8, but leave it blank.

GROUP TIME
1. If a skit fits the tone of your group, open with the skit described above.
   Alternate opening: What kinds of *why* questions do small children ask? Why might you limit the information you would give in answering a child's *why* questions?
2. What reasons might God have for choosing not to answer some of our *why* questions?
3. Look again at Satan's accusation in Job 1:9-11 and 2:4-5. Why were Satan's remarks about Job's motives such a serious charge?
4. If God had chosen to explain to Job the reason for his suffering, what do you think God would have said?
5. If you had been Job, would you have been satisfied with that explanation? With *any* explanation?
6. Job's wife (in her only line from a whole book of dialogue) said, "Do you still hold fast to your integrity? Curse God and die!" What does this suggest about her view of Job's character? Of God's character?
7. Using the first cycle of speeches from Job's three friends, discuss the chart in question 8 on page 18. What differing views of God

79

did Job's friends reflect?

8. Work together to complete the outcome chart of question 10 on page 19.

9. When have you seen similar positive outcomes follow a period of hardship? (Give examples from your own experience or from the experience of people you know.)

10. What have you learned about yourself through these experiences? About God?

11. Divide into groups of two for ten minutes. Talk about your work in the *Taking It Home* section on pages 22-24. Pray for each other.

12. Come together for a closing prayer. Use some of the suggestions for prayer in the *Refinement* section on page 24.

Group Study 3

SINKING INTO DESPAIR

OBJECTIVE

To encourage each group member to examine her faith to evaluate its ability to endure trial.

LEADER PREPARATION

- ❦ Complete the *Sifting for Nuggets* section.
- ❦ Read the *Staking a Claim* section.
- ❦ Do at least one suggestion from the *Taking It Home* section.
- ❦ Find a favorite praise song on tape and bring it with you to the group time. You may want to find someone to lead the group in a short time of worship to begin the meeting.

GROUP TIME

1. Listen to a praise song on tape or sing praise songs with your group.
2. What circumstances make it hard for you to praise God?
3. Look at the acrostic P.A.I.N. on page 28. What other steps have you seen lead to despair?
4. Find the question marks in Job's speeches of chapters 7, 9, 10, and 12. What kinds of questions was Job asking about God?
5. How would you describe Job's frame of mind during those speeches?
6. What help do you think would be of value to a person who began to question God's goodness, or His justice, or His power?
7. What circumstances have led you to question some of the attributes that Scripture assigns to God?
8. If you have experienced a period of inner turmoil, what helped you to regain stability in your faith?
9. What are some sins that often need to be confessed after people experience a period of trial?
10. Job 42:16 says that Job saw his sons and his grandsons to the fourth generation. What do you think that Job told them about the trial era of his life?
11. What would you want your descendants or close friends to learn from your own trials?
12. Which project did you do in the *Taking It Home* section? What

did you learn about yourself? About God?

13. Pray the prayer of Ephesians 3:14-21. Mentally insert the name of someone else in your group.

SAVING OUR FAITH

OBJECTIVE
To find ways to actively help our faith grow.

LEADER PREPARATION
- 🐛 Complete the *Sifting for Nuggets* section.
- 🐛 Read the *Staking a Claim* section.
- 🐛 Do at least one of the *Taking It Home* suggestions. Read the rest of them.
- 🐛 Make a picture of a staircase like the one below.

HUSHED
GOD SEEKING
IMMOVABLE FAITH
HONEST
PRAISE
ACCEPTANCE
INNER STRUGGLE
NEGATIVE ATTITUDE
SIN

- 🐛 Make a chart or handout with the following information.
  Sin: 1 John 1:9; 2 Peter 3:9; Job 40:1-2
  Negative Attitude: Psalm 96:7-10; Psalm 104:1; Job 12:12
  Inner Struggle: James 1:5; 2 Timothy 3:16-17; Job 33:13-14
  Acceptance: Romans 8:28; Jeremiah 29:11; Job 2:10
  Praise: Hebrews 13:15; Ephesians 5:19-20; Job 1:20-21
  Honest: Hebrews 4:14-15; Psalm 139:23-24; Job 7:11
  Immovable Faith: 1 Peter 1:6-7; Ephesians 6:10-11; Job 6:10
  God Seeking: Jeremiah 29:13; Hebrews 11:6; Job 13:15-16
  Hushed: Psalm 62:5; Psalm 46:10; Isaiah 30:21
- 🐛 Cut heavy paper into strips that can be used as bookmarks. Gather felt pens, decorative stamps, pressed flowers, yarn, clear adhesive paper, scissors, or anything you can think of to decorate bookmarks. Each member will make a bookmark during the study.

GROUP TIME

1. Study the staircase of growing faith. Even though our lives have some measure of each step in the staircase, our trend is usually moving either up or down. Notice that "praise" and "honest" appear near the middle of the staircase. Do you think that it is possible to be fully honest with God and still praise Him at the same time? Explain.

2. What inhibits us from being open with other people during our difficult times?

3. Read Job 7:16; 9:27-31; 30:24-28. What feelings did Job express to the Lord?

4. What emotions are hard to express to God?

5. Read Job 10:12; 12:13-18; 19:25-27. What are some basic beliefs that Job never let go?

6. What are some beliefs that you feel you would never let go?

7. Do you think that it is harder to believe in God during a time of suffering? Why, or why not?

8. Job was seeking God to the best of his ability, given his situation. What are some ways that we can seek God?

9. As you studied various passages of Scripture this week, what verse or verses stand out in your mind as texts that might help you maintain your faith during a time of hardship? Explain your choice.

10. Hebrew families sometimes created "rock piles" to remind themselves and their children of critical times in their lives when God had instructed them, or rescued them, or otherwise made Himself evident in their lives. They used these rock piles in times of suffering to remind themselves of God's strength and continued presence. What "rock pile" events in your life would help you remember God's presence with you in the past?

11. Notice the Scripture verses printed with the steps in the preparation section. Choose a verse that would help you maintain your faith in your own current circumstances. Make a bookmark that incorporates that verse along with your own creative expressions of its content. Keep the bookmark in your Bible or in some other place where it will see frequent use.

12. Read Colossians 1:9-14 as a closing prayer. Mentally insert the name of someone you know who is trying to maintain faith in spite of suffering.

Group Study 5

SERVING THE SUFFERER

OBJECTIVE

To actively seek to meet the needs of friends who are suffering.

LEADER PREPARATION

 🌟 Complete the *Sifting for Nuggets* section.

 🌟 Read the *Staking a Claim* section.

 🌟 Do at least one activity from the *Taking It Home* section.

 🌟 Familiarize yourself with the exercise in GROUP TIME. Create several other situations like the example in GROUP TIME suggestion number 13.

 🌟 Write the following questions on a large sheet of paper:
What is daily life like for her right now?
What might some of her fears be?
What are some of her new experiences?
What is her biggest pressure?
What is she spending most of her time doing?
What might be some of her physical, spiritual, and emotional needs?

 🌟 Bring several pairs of women's shoes and many small slips of paper to the group time.

GROUP TIME

1. Read aloud the first six paragraphs of *Staking a Claim*. What are some of the things that Ellen did that helped the author?

2. Read Job 2:11-13. What initial steps did Job's three friends take to comfort him?

3. How can we demonstrate patience with hurting friends?

4. What are some ways that we try to make our friends heal according to our own time table?

5. Review some of the harsh words between Job and his friends. From Eliphaz: Job 15:5-6; from Bildad: Job 8:3-4; from Zophar: Job 11:5-6; from Job: Job 19:2-3; 21:34. What do you think went wrong in the conversation that had been meant to comfort Job?

6. In what subtle ways might we mock or insult our own hurting friends, if we are not careful?

7. Read Job 13:3-5 for Job's perspective of his friend's words. What

are the dangers of speaking too much even if we say the right thing?

8. Read Job 6:14. How can a Christian affect a friend's spiritual condition?

9. Read Job's words in the following verses: Job 7:5; 13:5-6; 17:6; 19:16; 30:18; 30:30. What practical help could one of Job's friends have given him at each point?

10. Why do you think that Job's friends did not serve him in these practical ways?

11. Think of a time when your own life was particularly difficult. What acts of service came from your circle of acquaintances?

12. Read Job 16:4-5 and Ephesians 4:29. What statements have believing friends made to you that built you up in a time of need?

13. Put yourself in Sally's shoes. Set a pair of shoes on your table. Here is the person who walks in these shoes: Sally is a Christian who has three children, ages 2, 5, and 8. She has always stayed at home with them. Her husband has just left her and asked her for a divorce.

    Let each person take a slip of paper and answer several of the questions regarding Sally. (See PREPARATION.) Place these answers in Sally's shoes. Now ask a member of the group to read the slips of paper as you all try to get a picture of Sally's needs.

    Draw on your study of Job to discuss how you could help "Sally" in tactful, practical ways.

    If time permits, create several other "Sallys" with differing sets of circumstances.

Group Study 6

SENDING THE SUFFERER TO GOD

OBJECTIVE

To gain sensitivity and knowledge to help us communicate with people who suffer.

LEADER PREPARATION

- ❦ Complete the *Sifting for Nuggets* section.
- ❦ Complete at least one suggestion from the *Taking It Home* section.
- ❦ Read *Staking a Claim*.
- ❦ Using two sheets of paper, create and cut out two crosses with the captions below:

Cross A

```
                1 God
                  is
                  just
2 God    3 God    4 God
punishes   rewards    is
  the      the      good
 wicked  righteous
         5 God
           is
          mighty
         6 God
           is
          holy
```

Cross B

```
                1 God
                  is
                  just
2 God    3 God    4 God
  is       is       is
 love     mighty    good
         5 God
           is
          holy
         6 God
           is
          larger
          than
          our
          compre-
          hension
```

GROUP TIME

1. What unwanted advice have you received or seen someone else receive? What was the intention of that advice?

87

2. Read Job 32:1-10. What reasons did Elihu have for the timing and content of his speech?
3. Under what circumstances do you think you ought to give advice?
4. What are some situations where you think you ought to keep any potential advice to yourself?
5. Read Proverbs 27:5-6; 29:20, 23; 30:5-6. What wisdom do these verses add to the topic of giving advice? (Discuss each passage.)
6. What attitudes in a person make you unwilling to take his or her advice?
7. Think of a time when you didn't want to listen to anyone, yet someone got through to you. What caused you to listen?
8. Read each of these speech excerpts. Zophar: Job 11:1-6; Eliphaz: Job 15:1-6; Elihu: Job 33:31-33. If you had been commanded to listen silently to each of these people, what would you be thinking during each speech?
9. What are some advantages of learning by answering questions rather than by being told directly?
10. What advice did Elihu give Job? (See Job 35:14b; 36:18, 21, 24; 37:14.)
11. Study Elihu's words in Job 35:5-10. What all was Elihu trying to teach Job about God?
12. How can we help our own friends to see God with a larger perspective?
13. Notice the two crosses constructed in Number 4 of the PREPARATION. What is the difference between these two crosses?

    Instructions: Cross A shows some of the beliefs about God expressed by Job's first three friends. Fold this cross into the shape of a box. Cross B shows the beliefs about God expressed throughout Scripture. Fold this cross into a box, but leave the *bottom flap open.* (The bottom flap says that God is beyond our comprehension.) Study the results.

    How might "putting God in a box" affect your spiritual development?
14. Read aloud Elihu's statement in Job 36:26. Make one statement about God that expresses your own picture of God's greatness.
15. Pray for each other. Ask God to make you sensitive and wise in helping friends who are in pain.

SAVIOR'S ANSWERS

OBJECTIVE

To gain awareness of how Jesus meets our emotional and spiritual needs.

LEADER PREPARATION

❧ Complete the Sifting for Nuggets section.
❧ Read the Staking a Claim section.
❧ Do at least one suggestion from the Taking It Home section.
❧ Copy the following chart onto a large sheet of paper. Use this for discussion during your first questions of GROUP TIME.

GOD'S GOODNESS	QUESTIONS
Land Formations	Does God destroy hope? Job 14:18-22; Job 38:4-7
Light/Darkness	Does God use darkness to confuse us? Job 19:7-8; Job 38:12-15
Storms	Does God use His power to hurt us? Job 30:21-23; Job 38:25-27
Lion	Must we cower before God? Job 10:16; Job 38:39-40
Donkey	Does God cause oppression? Job 24:1-5; Job 39:5-10
Ostrich (Owl)	Does God treat us as mere animals? Job 30:28-29; Job 39:13-15
Eagle	Does God care that my life is slipping away? Job 9:25-26; Job 39:27-30

GROUP TIME

1. What do you find mysterious about God?
2. Using the passages listed above, study Job's implied question

and God's response regarding each area of creation listed in the chart. Even though God did not always give a direct answer to Job's question, what information did He reveal that might help Job solve the dilemma himself? (Discuss each part of God's creation one by one.)

3. Why do you think God did not give Job precise answers to his complaints?

4. When has some aspect of God's creation raised questions about His character in your own mind?

5. How has God's creation helped you to know Him better?

6. Read the opening lines of God's second speech in Job 40:6-14. In view of this introduction, what topics would you expect God to address?

7. What does this introduction suggest about the difference between Job and God?

8. Scholars aren't certain just what animal the Behemoth and Leviathan represent. (Guesses run the gamut from dinosaurs to dolphins.) Read God's description of the Behemoth in Job 40:15-24 and the Leviathan in 41:1-2 and 12-26. Make a pencil sketch below showing your version of one of these animals.

9. Review your chart on Question 10 (page 57). How might the story of Job have been different if it had occurred after Christ's era on earth? (Treat each of Job's cries separately.)

10. Read aloud the *Empathizes with Us* section beginning on page 59. Which of Christ's experiences on earth closely touch your own life? How could His experience help you to endure your own circumstance with continued faith?

11. Read aloud Romans 8:34-39. How has Jesus answered some of your own cries of pain?
12. Close in prayer for one another. Ask God to make you more in tune with Christ's presence and to recognize the Lord's unexpected answers to your questions.

Group Study 8

SURVIVORS

OBJECTIVE

To renew broken relationships with others and with God.

LEADER PREPARATION

🐛 Complete the *Sifting for Nuggets* section.

🐛 Read *Staking a Claim*.

🐛 Complete at least one suggestion from *Taking It Home*.

🐛 Obtain a set of building blocks. Borrow a set from your church preschool class if necessary. Copy the following list onto a piece of paper. Cut the list up and tape one word or phrase on each block.

acceptance	confrontation	listening
anger	distrust	mutual interest
availability	expressed forgiveness	openness
bitterness	faithfulness	time
commitment	letting go of the past	trust
concern	friendliness	unconditional love
confession	kindness	willingness to forgive

GROUP TIME

1. Use the labeled blocks created in preparation activity above in the following ways:

🐛 **Build a relationship.** Put the foundational aspects of the relationship on the bottom of the tower. Add blocks to the tower according to their importance. When the tower is finished, knock it down. When a relationship is damaged, what is added to the debris that wasn't part of the relationship before?

🐛 **Now construct a relationship that is being rebuilt after suffering damage.** How does this tower differ from the first one?

🐛 **Build a tower that represents a relationship between God and a person.** What does God contribute? What does the person contribute?

93

❧ **Knock down this tower.** What would it take to rebuild this tower? How would you construct it?

Alternate Opening: What ingredients does it take to make a good relationship? What all has to happen for a broken relationship to be rebuilt?

2. Read Job's response to God's first speech in Job 40:3-5. In as few words as possible, restate what Job said.

3. Read Job's response to God's second speech in Job 42:1-6. What spiritual steps do you see?

4. Throughout the Book of Job, Job begged God to meet with him. What did Job gain from his audience with God?

5. When God finished speaking, Job repented. Why? (If you are not sure, suggest your best guess.)

6. When has your own experience with God changed you in some significant way?

7. Read Job 42:7-9. Why do you think God made the three friends bring their sacrifice to Job?

8. Review God's instructions in verses 7-9. Who do you think had the harder job? Job or his friends? Explain.

9. Read Job 42:10-17. What gifts did God give to Job? (Find all that you can.)

10. Read Job 19:13-19 and 42:10-11. Why is it so hard to accept the kindness of someone who has wronged us?

11. Review Job 2:9-10 and 19-17. If you were Job's wife, what would you want from Job once the two of you were finally alone? What would you have done for him?

12. Job was a righteous man, yet he lost all that he had—and God didn't even tell him why. One major lesson throughout the Book of Job is that there is no direct relationship between doing good and material reward. God does not *owe* us anything. Why, then, do you think that the book ends with Job being happy and prosperous?

13. Do you think that Job still grieved for what he had lost? Explain.

14. Think back to when you started the study of *Gold in the Ashes*. What blessings have you received from God since that time? (Include knowledge of God, spiritual growth, material blessings.)

15. Close with sentence prayers thanking God for these expressions of His kindness.